Maths Made Easy

by KATHLEEN PATERSON

Mental Arithmetic Tests

TEST WORKSHEETS
Year 4

EGON

EGON PUBLISHERS LTD
Royston Road, Baldock, Hertfordshire, SG7 6NW, England

First published in the United Kingdom in 1999
by Egon Publishers Ltd,
Royston Road, Baldock, Hertfordshire SG7 6NW, England

Maths Made Easy, Mental Arithmetic Tests,
Worksheets: Year 4
Copyright © Egon Publishers Ltd.,
and Kathleen Paterson, 1999

ISBN 1 899998 43 8

Cover origination by Climacs Imagin. Text origination by Partners In Style.
Printed for the publishers by Streets Printers, Royston Road, Baldock, Hertfordshire SG7 6NW, England

Teachers Notes

About the tests
The tests contain the requirements as outlined in the National Numeracy Strategy for Year 4. There is of course scope for the teacher to use discretion in their use and allow for differentiation. The questions in each test vary in difficulty. Some easier questions are deliberately placed between harder ones so that children do not become too disheartened. The tests gradually increase in difficulty over the year. The children should be encouraged to keep a record of their own achievements.

Contained within the tests are:-

Addition	Shape and space
Subtraction	Capacity
Multiplication	Algebra
Division	Factors
Money problems	Estimation
Time recognition and problems	Multi-stop problems
Data handling exercises	Decimals - Term 3

Organising the Tests
There are enough tests for 2 per week throughout the year. It would be advisable for the teacher to read one test to the children and use the tape for the second so that the children become used to an unfamiliar voice. Odd numbers should be read by the teacher even numbers are covered by the tapes.

Reading the test
N.B. The children should not be allowed to ask questions once the test has started.

• Measure the time interval between questions. Give 5 - 10 seconds normally, but 15 seconds for questions requiring data handling.

• Each question should be read twice giving the question number on the first reading only.

• Pause after reading the question for a second time giving the appropriate time interval before the next question.

• Tell the children to put their pencils down immediately at the end of the test.

Marking
The answers to each test are at the back of the book. 1 point only should be given for a correct answer. To be correct the children must remember to write any appropriate abbreviations (i.e. p for pence, £ for one pound, g for grams etc.) Please note that the tests have been written in worksheet form. This is so that the sheet can be used to go over the test and make teaching points, or repeat it for homework. It is also useful in this way for those pupils who need to see the questions. Pupils new to this type of test might find it easier and make faster progress if they, at first, tackle the worksheets going through them with explanations. They could then gradually be introduced to doing the tests mentally.

Dedication

To Chris Dugdale, a friend and colleague, who recently died of cancer while these books were being created.

Acknowledgments

With grateful thanks to:-
Daphne Watts of Partners in Style, for all her origination.
Jenny Humphrey, Deputy Head of Berkhamsted Preparatory school and qualified Ofsted Inspector for her advice and encouragement.
Gail Batchelder a Year 4 teacher at Berkhamsted Preparatory school for trialling initial versions of this book with her pupils.
Graham Paterson, my husband, for his support and proof reading abilities.
Juliet Morgan for trialling the booklets individually.
Year 4 pupils of St. Nicholas House School for inspiring early versions of these booklets in the first place!

Test 1   Date...........   Name...................

1.   Add together 5 and 7.   ☐

2.   Take 3 from 10.   ☐

3.   7 x 2 =   ☐

4.   Add 12 and 4.   ☐

5.   Share 12 sweets between 2 people. How many each?   ☐

6.   Put these in order smallest first:- 17, 21, 19   ☐ ☐ ☐

7.   6 + [   ] = 13   ☐

8.   Multiply 2 by 10.   ☐

9.   Write 37 in words.   ☐

10.   What is 4 more than 19?   ☐

11.   Draw the hands of the clock to show 5.30pm.

12.   Find the sum of 28 and 30.   ☐

13.   Write one hundred and six in figures.   ☐

14.   The scale shows the amount of water in the jug.

      How many litres are there in the jug?   ☐

15.   Kath eats one quarter of a pie. What fraction

      of the pie is left?   ☐

Test 2   Date........... Name.....................

1.   Add together 6 and 9.

2.   What is 20 take away 4?

3.   What are three lots of five?

4.   What is 8p less than 20p?

5.   Find half of 10.

6.   How many tens in thirty?

7.   Take 10 from 45.

8.   Write one hundred and twenty-four in figures.

9.   Write 640 in words.

10.   What is one less than 30?

11.   4 = [ ] - 10.

12.   How long is the pencil

       in centimetres?

13.   What is 56 rounded to the nearest 10?

14.   How many degrees in a right angle?

15.   Jack left home at 8.30am. He arrived at school at 8.56am.

       How many minutes did he take to get to school?

Test 3   Date........... Name....................

1. Find the sum of 3 and 9.

2. 16 - 9 =

3. 3 x 6 =

4. Share 12 into 3 lots. How many in each lot?

5. What is 4 + 3 + 2 + 1?

6. Add 10 to 31.

7. 5 + [ ] = 10

8. Write two hundred and twenty-six in numbers.

9. Multiply 4 by 10.

10. Rewrite the numbers in order, putting the smallest

    number first:-   41, 18, 21, 36

11. Write 507 in words.

12. What is 6 more than 48?

13. The table shows some children's

	girls	boys
dog	5	26
cat	38	21
rabbits	25	4

    favourite pets. How many like cats best?

14. How many tens in 80?

15. Draw in the hands of the clock to show 6.35pm.

Test 4   Date...........   Name...................

1.   Add 6 to 17.

2.   Take four from eleven.

3.   Estimate in degrees the size of angle 'A' on your sheet.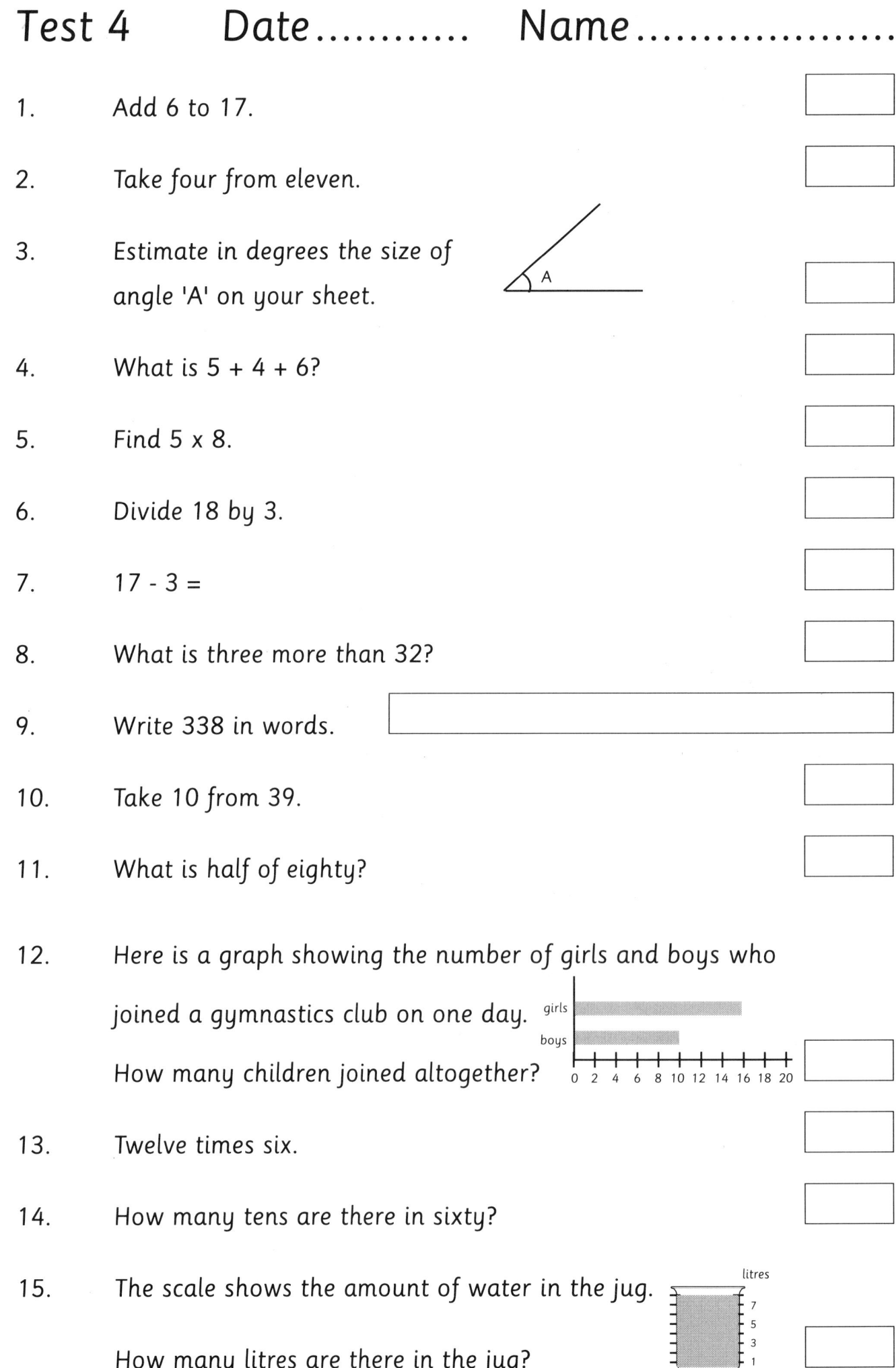

4.   What is 5 + 4 + 6?

5.   Find 5 x 8.

6.   Divide 18 by 3.

7.   17 - 3 =

8.   What is three more than 32?

9.   Write 338 in words.

10.   Take 10 from 39.

11.   What is half of eighty?

12.   Here is a graph showing the number of girls and boys who joined a gymnastics club on one day. How many children joined altogether?

13.   Twelve times six.

14.   How many tens are there in sixty?

15.   The scale shows the amount of water in the jug.

How many litres are there in the jug?

Test 5   Date........... Name....................

1. Find the sum of 7 and 3 and 5..   [ ]

2. Take 4 from 13.   [ ]

3. Share 15 pencils among 3 children. How many each?   [ ]

4. Add 2 + 4 + 6.   [ ]

5. Multiply 7 by 3.   [ ]

6. Write 137 in words.   [   ]

7. Add one to 39.   [ ]

8. Which is the smallest number?   34, 14, 27, 17, 20   [ ]

9. [ ] + (3 + 4) = 10   [ ]

10. Which is the largest number?   16, 116, 161   [ ]

11. There are four 20 pence and two 10 pence coins in a purse.

    How much money is there in the purse altogether?   [ ]

12. Take 10 from 30.   [ ]

13. Can you see an <u>odd</u> or <u>even</u> number of books? Tick the right box.   [odd] [even]

14. Write three hundred and sixty-seven in figures.   [ ]

15. What fraction of the square is shaded?   [ ]

Test 6   Date............   Name....................

1. Write the time as it would appear on a digital clock. [clock image]   [ ]

2. Add together 4 and 9 and 6.   [ ]

3. Take 8 from 20.   [ ]

4. Add 7p to 12p.   [ ]

5. 6 x 7 =   [ ]

6. Two lots of 6 make . . . ?   [ ]

7. 10 - [   ] = 2.   [ ]

8. Write 339 in words.   [   ]

9. Take one from 20.   [ ]

10. Take 10 from 47.   [ ]

11. Put these in order, with the largest

    number first:-   21, 27, 17, 13   [ ] [ ] [ ] [ ]

12. It took Jan from 5.15pm to 6.30pm to finish her work.

    How many hours and minutes did it take her?   [   ]

13. How many lines of symmetry can be drawn   [ ]

    on the shape shown?   [ ]

14. Divide 48 by 8.   [ ]

15. Add £1.50 and £2.30.   [ ]

Test 7　　Date........... Name.....................

1.　　Add together 5 and 10 and 3.　　☐

2.　　Take 9 from 17.　　☐

3.　　What are three lots of twelve?　　☐

4.　　3 x 4 =　　☐

5.　　What is half of 14?　　☐

6.　　Write 248 in words.　　☐

7.　　10 = (4 + 2) + ☐　　☐

8.　　5 x 10 =　　☐

9.　　Take one from 40.　　☐

10.　　Add ten to twelve.　　☐

11.　　Each glass holds 50 mls of Coke.

　　　How many millilitres do ten glasses hold?　　☐

12.　　Sam pays for his 25p toy with a £1 coin.

　　　How much change does he get?　　☐

13.　　What time should the clock show in

　　　thirty minutes time?　　☐

14.　　What is two less than 650?　　☐

15.　　What fraction of the square is shaded?　　☐

Test 8   Date...........   Name....................

1.   Add together 7 and 9 and 3.   `19`

2.   Take 5 from 19.   `14`

3.   3 x 8 =   `24`

4.   Find $^1/_2$ of 16.   `8`

5.   If one toffee costs 3p, how much do 7 toffees cost?   `21`

6.   10 - [ ] = 8   `2`

7.   Take 10 from 136.   `126`

8.   Which two numbers add up to 10?   7, 4, 8, 3, 5   `4` `3`

9.   What is 3 more than 10?   `13`

10.   Make 3 ten times bigger.   `30`

11.   What shape is made if the dots on the square

   are joined? Tick the correct word. | square | circle | triangle | rectangle |

12.   What is half of 62?

13.   How many 20p coins make £1?

14.   The chart shows boys and girls who joined

   the gymnastic club on one day. How many more

   girls joined the gymnastic club than boys?

15.   Divide 36 by 12.

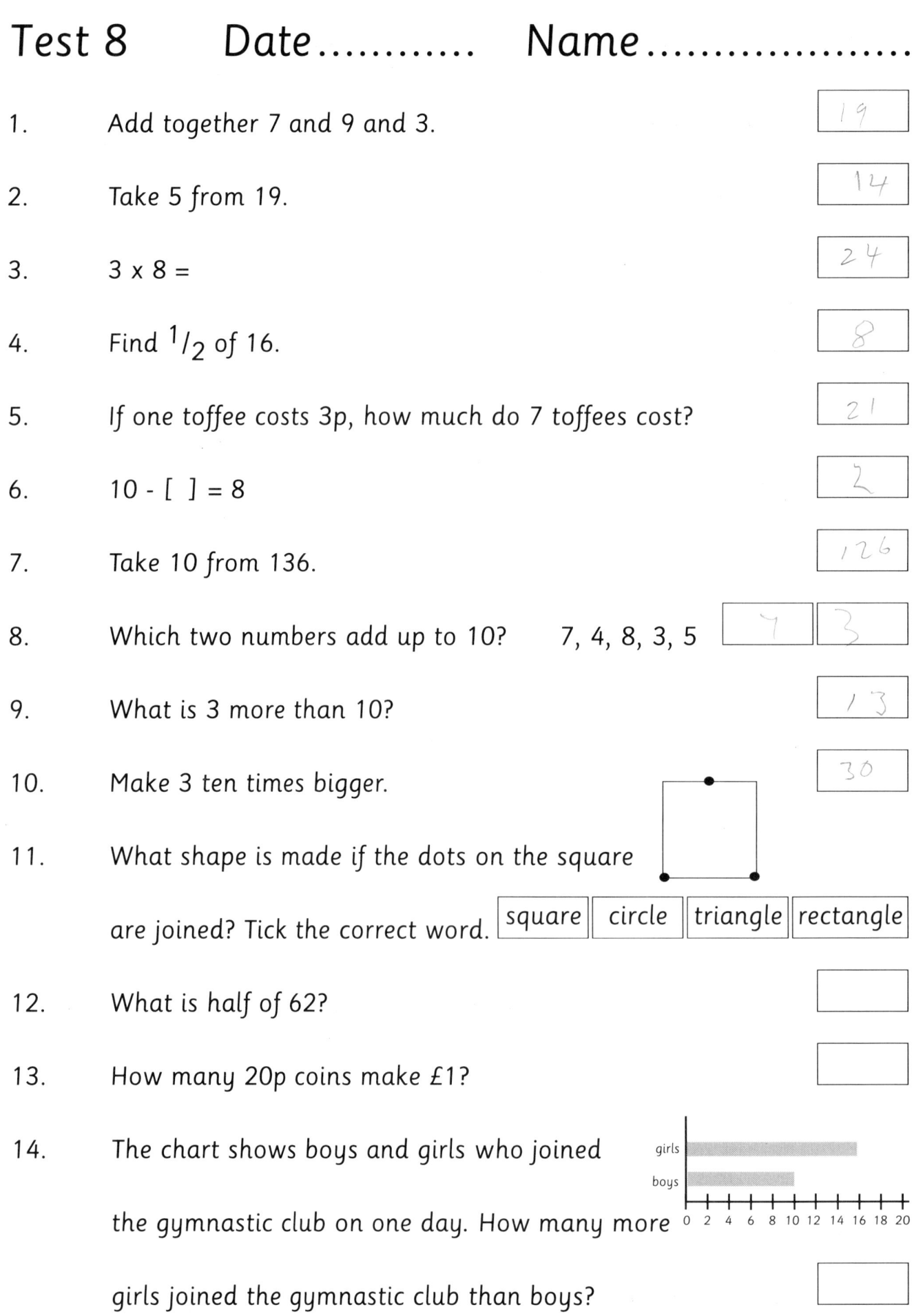

Test 9   Date.......... Name.....................

1.   Add together 4 and 8 and 7. ☐

2.   15 - 7 = ☐

3.   Find 9 lots of 2. ☐

4.   The table shows the number of coloured pencils in Don's pencil case. How many pencils did Don have in his case altogether?

	coloured pencils
brown	7
red	6
green	4

☐

5.   What is half of 20? ☐

6.   Write 487 in words. ☐

7.   Take 10 from 34. ☐

8.   (1 + 1) + ☐ = 12 ☐

9.   Take three from twenty-six. ☐

10.   Draw the hands of the clock to show 8:45am.

11.   Put in order, the smallest first:-

99, 170, 213, 43, 18   ☐ ☐ ☐ ☐ ☐

12.   Divide 48 by 6. ☐

13.   Add 9p to 11p. ☐

14.   A can of Coke cost 80p and a bag of apples cost 97p. How much do the can of Coke and the apples cost altogether? ☐

15.   Write five hundred and five pence in pounds and pence. ☐

Test 10   Date............   Name......................

1.   Add together 5 and 9 and 3.   ☐

2.   What is 14 take away 8?   ☐

3.   Find $^1/_2$ of 12p.   ☐

4.   The diagram represents square cms.

      How many square cms are shaded?   ☐

5.   Add one to 44.   ☐

6.   Write nine hundred and forty-six in numbers.   ☐

7.   Which is the largest number in this list?

      102, 123, 145, 213, 312   ☐

8.   100 - 2 =   ☐

9.   Add 6p and 12p and 3p.   ☐

10.   Take 10 from 27.   ☐

11.   3 x 6 =   ☐

12.   Ring the largest fraction. $^1/_2$ $^3/_4$ $^2/_3$ $^1/_3$

13.   What is the next multiple of 8?   8, 16, 24   ☐

14.   £4.32 + £0.56   ☐

15.   How many right angles can you see on the front of a book?   ☐

Test 11   Date............   Name....................

1.   What is the sum of 11 and 8?

2.   What is 16 take away 7?

3.   What is 3 + 5 + 4 + 1?

4.   Estimate the position of the arrow to

the nearest decade.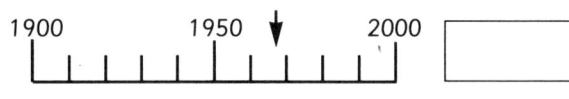

5.   Share 18 sweets among 3 children.

6.   [ ] + 2 = 18

7.   How many tens are there in 50?

8.   What is ten more than 26?

9.   4 x [ ] = 40

10.   Put these in order, smallest first:-

16, 11, 14, 10

11.   Draw the hands of the clock to show 7:55.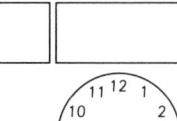

12.   Multiply 4 by 4.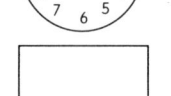

13.   What is 3^2?

14.   What is the perimeter of the shape shown?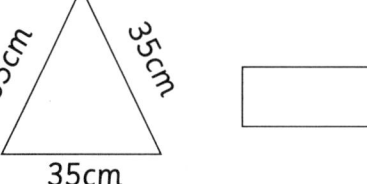

15.   A cake is divided into 9 equal slices. If 3 people eat the

same number of slices what fraction does one person eat?

Test 12   Date............   Name....................

1. Add together 5 and 8 and 2.

2. 15 - 8 =

3. What are 3 lots of 8?

4. Which lines total 1 metre?   _____26cm_____
   _____46cm_____
   _____23cm_____
   Write the answer as a sum. _____54cm_____

5. What is half of 16?

6. What is 1 more than 29?

7. What is 10 more than 34?

8. Write 132 in words.

9. 15 - [ ] = 6

10. How many tens in 70?

11. Identical shapes have the same value.

    What is the value of

    the banana?

    total 75   total 45

    total 85

12. Add 5p to 12p.

13. How many 2p coins make 20p?

14. Which 3 coins make the sum of £1.55?

15. What weight is shown
    on the scale?   200g   300g   400g

Test 13   Date............   Name.....................

1.   Add together 5 and 6 and 3.

2.   Take seven from eleven and add 1.

3.   Add 9p to 11p.

4.   The chart shows the scores of Sarah's last 3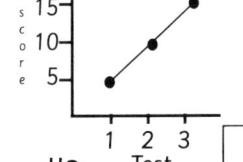

   mental tests. By how many did she improve overall?

5.   Find two lots of 11p.

6.   10 - [   ] = 4

7.   Take one from 40.

8.   Write one hundred and six in numbers.

9.   Put in order with the largest first:-

   15, 6, 39, 103, 42

10.   Take 10 from 77.

11.   Add the numbers on the adjacent boxes to find

   the number at the top.

12.   £6.74 + £2.03

13.   2 x 12 =

14.   Write the time as it would appear on a digital clock.

15.   What is the perimeter of a square with sides 5 cm long?

Test 14   Date............   Name...................

1.   Add together 6 and 9.   ▢

2.   From 17 take 8.   ▢

3.   What are 5 lots of 6?   ▢

4.   4 x 4 =   ▢

5.   What is $^1/_2$ of 22?   ▢

6.   Write 157 in words.   [   ]

7.   (10 - 3) + 4 =   ▢

8.   Take 3 from 50.   ▢

9.   5 x 12 =   ▢

10. Add 10 to 43.   ▢

11. The number in the circle is the total of two   ㉝

     consecutive numbers. Write the numbers.   ▢ ▢

12. How many minutes did John take to drive to his

     friends if he left at 3.30pm and arrived at 4.15pm?   ▢

13. Round £6.18 to the nearest £1.   ▢

14. Write the number shown on the

     abacus in figures.   h   t   u   ▢

15. What is the time half an hour later than 7.45pm?   ▢

Test 15   Date............   Name...................

1.   What is the sum of 8 and 9?

2.   19 - 8 =

3.   Multiply 4 by 3.

4.   Share 27 between 3.

5.   Add together 8p and 12p.

6.   4 + [   ] + 5 = 15

7.   Put these in order, largest first:-

        41, 213, 7, 25

8.   Take 2 from 28.

9.   4 x [   ] = 36

10.   Add ten to 36.

11.   James has £1.50 and Mick has 75p. How much more

        does James have than Mick?

12.   Write the time as it would appear on a digital clock.

13.   What is one hour earlier than the time shown

        on the clock?

14.   9 x 6 = [   ]

15.   What is the difference in cms

        shown by the arrows?

Test 16   Date........... Name....................

1.   Find the sum of 9 and 3 and 2.

2.   Take 5 from 13.

3.   Share 21 among 3.

4.   The scale shows the amount of water in the jug.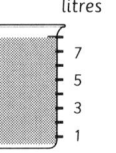

     How many litres of water are in the jug?

5.   Multiply 4 by 6.

6.   Write two hundred and ninety-three in figures.

7.   Which is the smallest number?   34, 15, 28, 32, 19

8.   Add two to thirty-nine. Answer in words.

9.   Take 10 from 20.

10. ☐ + (6 + 7) = 20

11. Estimate the size in degrees of the
     angle shown.

12. Which is the largest number?   16, 116, 611, 161

13. What is the next number in the sequence? 36, 40, 44, 48

14. What is 5 plus 4 plus 8?

15. What is the distance

     from A to B?

Test 17   Date........... Name....................

1.   Find the total of 4 and 12 and 7.

2.   Take 9 from 20.

3.   John drove from A to D.

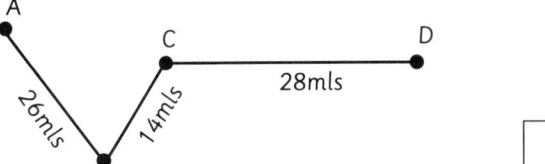

      How far did he travel?

4.   Multiply 12 by 4.

5.   Share 28 into 4 groups.

6.   Take 10 from the largest number:-   43, 54, 45, 53

7.   Add one to 79.

8.   What is the value of the 6 in 69?

9.   10 x 4 =

10.   Which is the odd number shown?   92, 56, 24, 38, 53, 70

11.   26 - [   ] = 19

12.   The diagram represents square

      centimetres. What is the area of the

      shaded part in square centimetres?

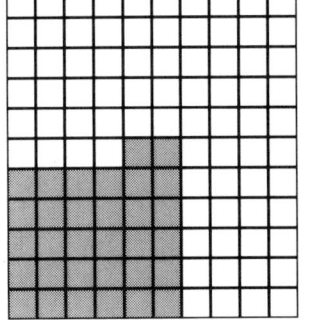

13.   Add 16 and 10.

14.   How many 5p coins in 60 pence?

15.   How many degrees in half a right angle?

Test 18   Date.......... Name...................

1. Find the total of 6, 7 and 8. ☐

2. 13 - 4 = ☐

3. Share 14 sweets between a couple of children.

    How many sweets each? ☐

4. What is three times seven? Answer in words. ☐

5. Add together 3p, 6p and 11p. ☐

6. Write 2,103 in words. ☐

7. How many tens are there in 50? ☐

8. 10 - [   ] = 3. ☐

9. Write the number shown on

    the abacus in figures.   Th   h   t   u   ☐

10. Which two numbers add up to 14? 4, 3, 8, 5, 6, 7 ☐ ☐

11. 22 - 5 = ☐

12. Put these numbers in order. Start with the smallest.

    1,156, 56, 1,056, 156   ☐ ☐ ☐ ☐

13. Three-fifths of the pages in a book have pictures.

    What fraction do not have pictures? ☐

14. What number is one more than 1,569? ☐

15. Write the time as it would appear on a digital clock. ☐

Test 19   Date............   Name....................

1.   Add together eight and eight.   ☐

2.   Take 5 from 29.   ☐

3.   Write the number shown on the abacus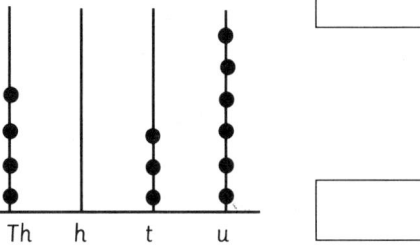

   in figures.   ☐

4.   What is the value of the 5 in 576?   ☐

5.   If one toffee costs 10p, how much do four toffees cost?   ☐

6.   14 - [   ] = 4   ☐

7.   Take 10 from 52.   ☐

8.   Which two numbers add up to 13?   2, 3, 7, 4, 6   ☐ ☐

9.   What is 10 more than 99?   ☐

10.   Which number is two less than 2,671?   ☐

11.   12 x 4 =   ☐

12.   Susan drove from A to F. How much

   further did she have to go after she arrived at C?   ☐

13.   3 x 6 =   ☐

14.   Write 5,267 in words.   ☐

15.   Round £5.28 to the nearest pound.   ☐

Test 20   Date........... Name.................

1.   Add together 6 metres and 11 metres.

2.   Take six from twenty.

3.   Share nine among three. How many each?

4.   What are a couple of eights?

5.   Sophie has 8 dolls and Mary has 12.

     How many dolls are there altogether?

6.   How many tens are there in 90?

7.   Put in order with the smallest first:-

     98, 47, 2, 120, 13.

8.   What is the value of the 3 in 473?

9.   Write 367 in words.

10. 7 x [   ] = 77

11. A coat cost £28.40. If there was a half price sale,

     how much would the coat cost?

12. What is the size in degrees of angle B?

13. What is the size in degrees of angle A?

14. Take 10 from 1,187.

15. Write the time as it would appear on a digital clock.

Test 21   Date........... Name....................

1.   What is the total of 15p and 9p?

2.   29 - 2 =

3.   (10 - 2) + 6 =

4.   Which is the even number?   7, 63, 20, 59, 45

5.   The scale shows the amount of water in a jug.
      How many more litres would be needed to fill
      the jug to the top mark?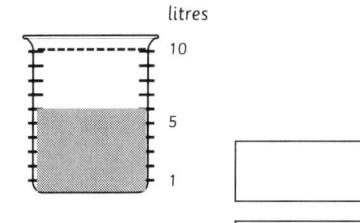

6.   Add 10 to 89.

7.   Take 10 from 34.

8.   Share 66 among 11.

9.   Write 3,584 in words.

10.   Multiply 11 by 3.

11.   What is 100 less than 6,710?

12.   Write the number shown on the

      abacus in figures.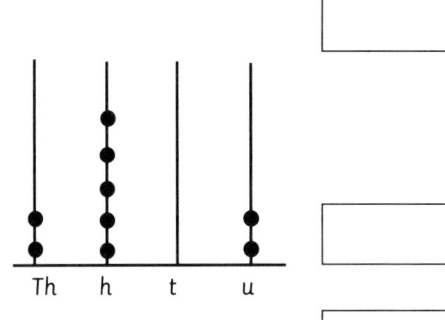

13.   How many fives in 60?

14.   Find 3 x 9.

15.   What fraction of the equilateral triangle
      is shaded?

Test 22   Date........... Name.....................

1.   What is 25 take away 6?

2.   Take 25p away from £1.00.

3.   I have 20p to spend and I buy some sweets for 15p.
     How much do I have left?

4.   The chart shows the number of bricks that
     builders A and B used to repair a wall.
     How many bricks were used altogether?

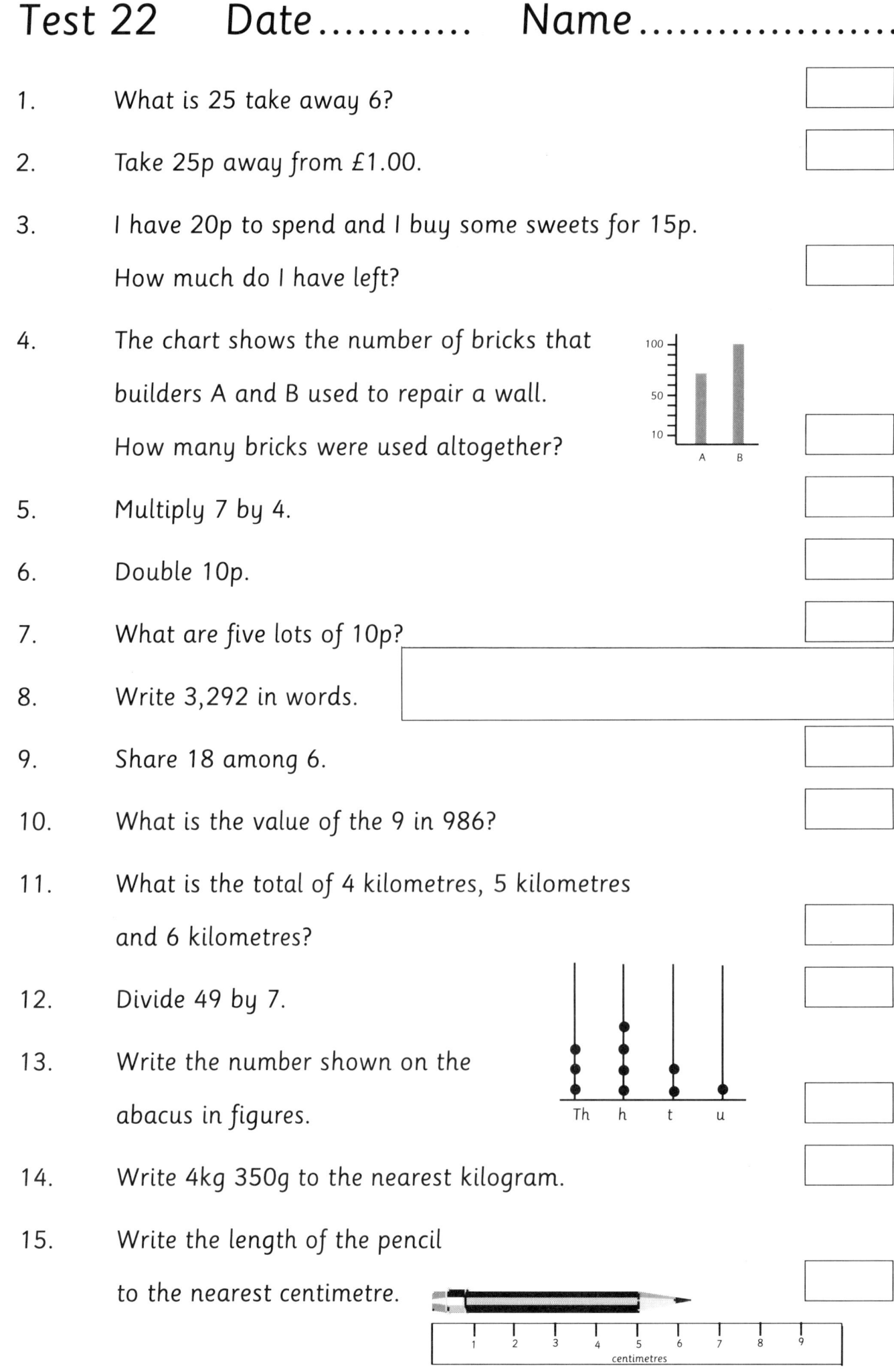

5.   Multiply 7 by 4.

6.   Double 10p.

7.   What are five lots of 10p?

8.   Write 3,292 in words.

9.   Share 18 among 6.

10. What is the value of the 9 in 986?

11. What is the total of 4 kilometres, 5 kilometres
     and 6 kilometres?

12. Divide 49 by 7.

13. Write the number shown on the
     abacus in figures.

14. Write 4kg 350g to the nearest kilogram.

15. Write the length of the pencil
     to the nearest centimetre.

Test 23   Date........... Name....................

1. Find the sum of 4 and 13. ☐

2. What is 9 less than 20? ☐

3. I have 50p and spend 42p. How much do I have left? ☐

4. Find seven lots of three. ☐

5. What is the value of 7 in 796? ☐

6. ☐ + (6 + 3) = 10 ☐

7. What is one less than 70? ☐

8. Multiply 12 by 4. ☐

9. If one toy costs 9p, what do 3 toys cost? ☐

10. Write two thousand, one hundred and seventy-three in figures. ☐

11. Divide 3,100 by 10. ☐

12. What is the perimeter of the shape? ☐

30cm · 50cm · 40cm

13. Ros correctly spelt 6 out of 10 words. What fraction of the total is this? ☐

14. Mark started work at 9.15am and spent 3 hours before stopping. At what time did he stop? ☐

15. Write the weight shown by the arrow. ☐

200g   300g   400g

Test 24   Date............   Name....................

1.   Add eleven to seven.

Answer in words.

2.   From 17 take 8.

3.   Draw the hands of the clock to show 11:45.

4.   Oranges cost 6p each. How many can you buy for 18p?

5.   Share 16 into 4 groups. How many in each group?

6.   10p + 7p + 3p =

7.   [   ] - 3 = 7

8.   100 - 1 =

9.   Write 538 in words.

10.   What is the value of 9 in 389?

11.   What is three score years and ten?

12.   Write the number shown on the

abacus in figures.

Th   h   t   u

13.   What is a couple of dozen?

14.   Add 40p to £5.90.

15.   Write the weight shown by the arrow

on the scale.

600g   700g   800g

Test 25   Date.......... Name....................

1.   Find the sum of 7 and 3 and 8.

2.   Take 4 from 13.

3.   The chart shows the arrival times

Arrivals			
Flight	From	Due	Landed
BA214	Boston	8.45am	10.16am
BA108	Boston	6.20am	9.35am

of the flights from Boston. How late

was the BA108?

4.   Add 2 + 4 + 6 + 4

5.   Multiply 7 by 8.

6.   Write 1,236 in words.

7.   Add one to 39.

8.   Take one from 30.

9.   ☐ + (3 + 4) = 10

10.   Which is the smallest number?   34, 14, 27, 17, 13

11.   Share 15 among 3.

12.   146 + 20 = [   ]

13.   Write the number shown on the abacus

      in figures.

14.   Jane had £5.60 in her purse. She gave her son £1.20.

      How much did she have left in her purse?

15.   Which is the largest number?   3163, 1683, 8631

Test 26   Date........... Name...................

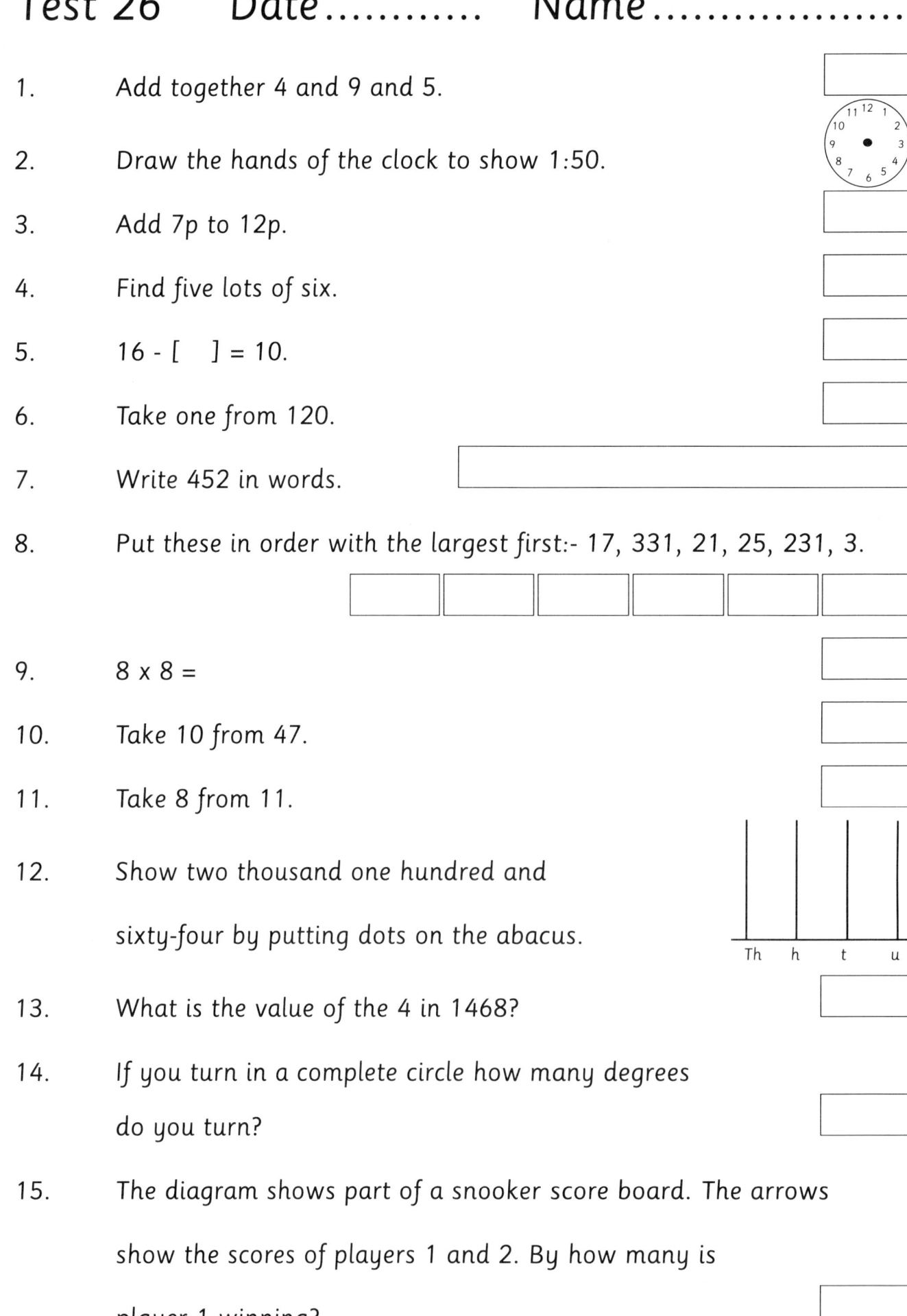

1.   Add together 4 and 9 and 5.

2.   Draw the hands of the clock to show 1:50.

3.   Add 7p to 12p.

4.   Find five lots of six.

5.   16 - [   ] = 10.

6.   Take one from 120.

7.   Write 452 in words.

8.   Put these in order with the largest first:- 17, 331, 21, 25, 231, 3.

9.   8 x 8 =

10.   Take 10 from 47.

11.   Take 8 from 11.

12.   Show two thousand one hundred and

       sixty-four by putting dots on the abacus.

13.   What is the value of the 4 in 1468?

14.   If you turn in a complete circle how many degrees

       do you turn?

15.   The diagram shows part of a snooker score board. The arrows

       show the scores of players 1 and 2. By how many is

       player 1 winning?

Test 27   Date........... Name...................

1.   Find the sum of 3 and 9 and 9.

2.   16 - 9 =

3.   6 x 12 =

4.   Share 35 into 7 lots. How many in each lot?

5.   What is 4 + 3 + 7 + 2?

6.   Show two thousand three hundred and seven

      by drawing dots on the abacus.

      Th   h   t   u

7.   17 - [   ] = 8.

8.   Write 726 in words.

9.   Multiply 4 by 6.

10.   Rewrite in order putting the smallest first:-

      41, 49, 7, 111, 12.

11.   Six vases each had 9 flowers in them.
      How many flowers altogether?

12.   James walked 13 kilometres and Susan walked
      18 kilometres. What is the difference in the distances
      they walked in kilometres?

13.   Subtract 9 from 18.

14.   Noreen bought 8 bread rolls for 9p each.
      How much did she spend?

15.   The diagram shows part of a snooker score board. The arrows
      show the scores of players 3 and 4. What is the difference
      in their scores?

      Player 3
      0• 1• 2• 3• 4• 5• 6• 7• 8• 9• 10• 11• 12• 13• 14• 15• 16• 17• 18• 19• 20   0• 20• 40• 60• 80• 100
      Player 4

Test 28   Date........... Name.....................

1.   Add 6 and 5 to 8.

2.   Take 5 from 11.

3.   What is 5 + 4 + 6?

4.   Write the time as it would appear on a digital clock.

5.   Share 81 among 9.

6.   How many tens are there in 120?

7.   14 - 3 =

8.   Write 1,898 in words.

9.   What is one more than 439?

10.   Take ten away from 39.

11.   7 x 9 =

12.   Write the number shown on the abacus

in figures.

Th   h   t   u

13.   What is 100 more than 578?

14.   The chart shows entry prices into the circus on different days.

How much would the entry cost be

	Adult	Child
Mon - Fri	£8.00	£4.50
Sat, Sun	£9.00	£5.50

for 2 adults and 1 child on Saturday?

20cm

15.   What is the perimeter of the rectangle?

8cm

Test 29   Date........... Name...................

1.   Add together 5 and 7 and 4 and 1.

2.   Take 4 from 15.

3.   Show one thousand and sixty-four by

     drawing dots on the abacus.

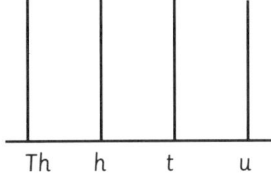

Th   h   t   u

4.   What is 11 + 7?

5.   Share 32 among 8.

6.   How many tens are there in 80?

7.   17 - [   ] = 13.

8.   Multiply 3 by 6.

9.   Write 74 in words.

10.   What is 1 more than 119?

11.   Shapes that are the same have the same

      number. What is the value of the carrot? total 48   total 44

      total 36

12.   What is the difference between 1,000 and 997?

13.   4 x 9 =

14.   One bat cost £1.03. How much for 3 bats?

15.   Write the weight in grams

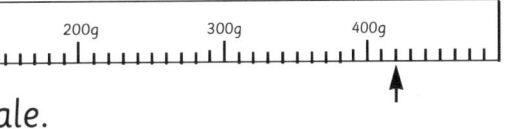

200g   300g   400g

      shown by the arrow on the scale.

Test 30   Date............   Name....................

1.   Add together 6 and 9 and 3.

2.   What is 20 take away 4?

3.   What are 6 lots of 5?

4.   Alex was facing E. If he turned through 180°
which way would he face?

5.   Find half of 10.

6.   How many tens are there in 140?

7.   Take ten from 45.

8.   What is one less than 70?

9.   4 + [   ] = 15

10.   Write eleven hundred and forty-six in figures.

11.   Ann drove from A to E. How far in
kilometres had she travelled when she arrived at D?

12.   What is 100 less than 1,563?

13.   What is 8p less than £1.20?

14.   If each dart in a game scores 20, how many
darts are needed to make 60?

15.   Write the number shown on the
abacus in figures.

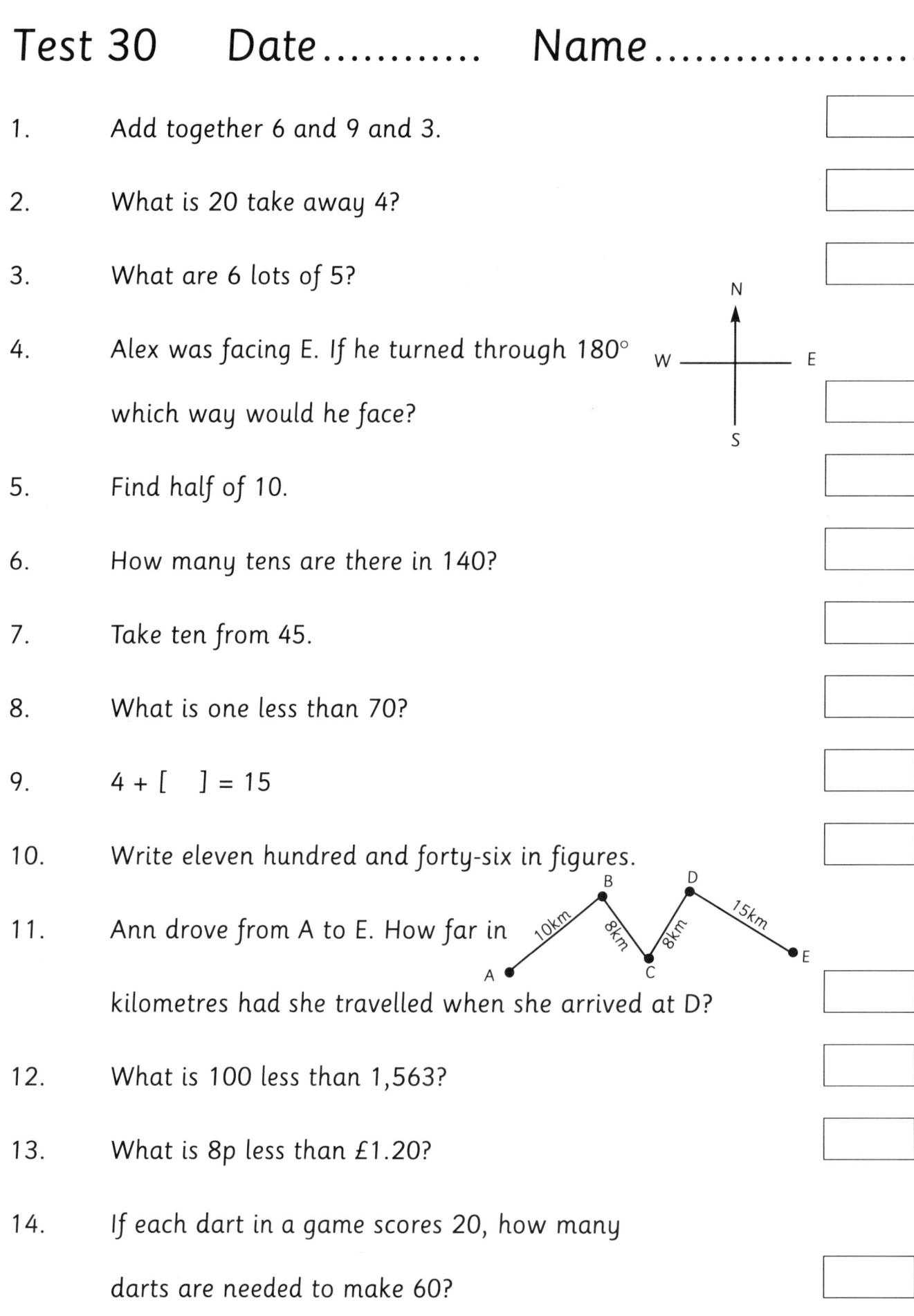

Test 31   Date........... Name....................

1. Find the sum of 7 and 8 and 6.

2. Alex is facing South, he turns 90° clockwise.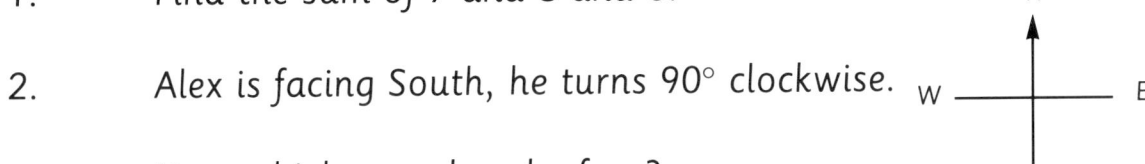

   Now which way does he face?

3. What is 3 + 4 + 5 + 6?

4. Multiply 12 by 4.

5. Share 18 by 3.

6. Put these in order with the smallest first:- 132, 16, 7, 128, 4, 1344

7. [   ] - 3 = 9

8. How many tens are there in 50?

9. What is ten more than 26?

10. 6 x [   ] = 42

11. Peter sets off at 8.10am and takes 45 minutes to

    cycle to school. What time does he arrive?

12. The dotted line on the scale shows the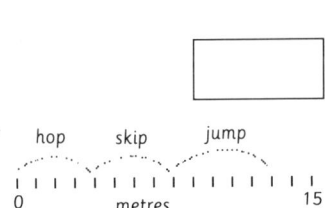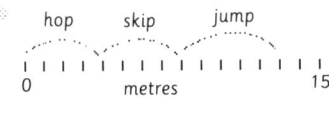

    distance Sam covered in the triple jump.

    How far did he jump altogether in metres?

13. How much change from £10 does Ian have if his

    ticket costs £6.50?

14. What is 16 take away 7?

15. Which is the biggest number?   3268, 3862, 3682

Test 32   Date............   Name....................

1.   Add together 5 and 8 and 3.

2.   15 - 8 =

3.   Draw the dots on the abacus to

show 4,862.

Th   h   t   u

4.   Add 5p to £2.13.

5.   What is two more than 34?

6.   Write 5,380 in words.

7.   10 take away [   ] = 4.

8.   How many tens are there in 70?

9.   What are 2 lots of 12?

10.   Write two thousand and seventy in figures.

11.   Write the time as it would appear on a digital clock.

12.   What is half of 16?

13.   What is one more than 89?

14.   Alex is facing West. He turns anti clockwise

N

W ——┼—— E

through 270°. Now which way does he face?

S

15.   What is 100 less than 2,656?

Test 33   Date........... Name.....................

1. Add together 9 and 7 and 6.

2. 15 - 7 =

3. Find 9 lots of 6.

4. Add 9p to £1.08, then take away 2p.

5. What is half of 14?

6. Write 3,218 in words.

7. What is the smallest number in this list? 33, 324, 22, 19, 90

8. Take 10 from 54.

9. 1 + [   ] + 3 = 12.

10. Write the number shown on the

    abacus in figures.

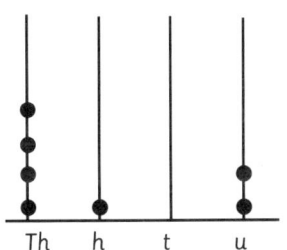

11. Which is the largest odd number?   667, 70, 143, 668

12. What is half an hour more than 11:50am?

13. Take one from 126.

14. Add 10 to 1,990.

15. Write the weight in grams shown by the arrow on the scale.

Test 34   Date........... Name....................

1.   Add together 5 and 9 and 8.

2.   What is 24 take away 8?

3.   Draw the hands on the clock to show 11:25am.

4.   6 x 3 =

5.   Add together 6p and 13p.

6.   Write four hundred and forty-six in numbers.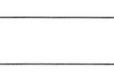

7.   Take one away from 243.

8.   Which is the largest number in this list?

      1243, 1234, 1245, 1236, 1326

9.   10 - [   ] = 3

10.   Take 10p away from 27p.

11.   Find half of 12.

12.   How many litres are there

      altogether in both jugs?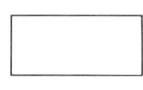

13.   Add 100 to 3,685.

14.   Nejat drinks 4 cups of tea a day.

      How many cups of tea does he drink in a week?

15.   Share 72 marbles between 9 children.

      How many marbles will each child have?

Test 35   Date........... Name...................

1. Add together 5 and 10.

2. Take 9 from 14.

3. What are 7 lots of 12?

4. 3 x 9 =

5. What is $\frac{1}{2}$ of 22?

6. Write 2,085 in words.

7. 10 = (4 + 2) + ☐

8. 5 x 10 =

9. Take one from 240.

10. Add ten to one hundred and twelve.

    Answer in words.

11. Jane caught a bus at 6.30pm. Her trip took 45 minutes.

    At what time did she arrive?

12. Write the weight shown

    600g   700g   800g

    by the arrow on the scale.

13. Share 49 sweets between 7 children.

    How many sweets does each child have?

14. Which is larger, 2860 or 2608?

15. The diagram shows part of a snooker score board. The arrows

    indicate the scores of players 1 and 2. How much more did

    Player 1 score? Player 1

    0• 1• 2• 3• 4• 5• 6• 7• 8• 9• 10• 11• 12• 13• 14• 15• 16• 17• 18• 19• 20   0• 20• 40• 60• 80• 100

    Player 2

Test 36   Date............   Name.....................

1.   Add together 7 and 9 and 7.

2.   Take 5 from 19, then add 1.

3.   8 x 4 =

4.   What is $^1/_2$ of 16?

5.   If one toffee costs 3p, what do seven toffees cost?

6.   12 - [   ] = 8

7.   Take 10 from 30.

8.   Which two numbers add up to 10?   7, 4, 5, 3, 8

9.   What is 3 more than 11?

10.   Make 4 ten times bigger.

11.   What is the perimeter of the pentagon?

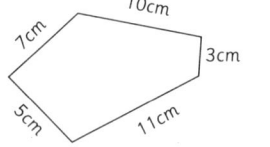

12.   Juliet has 72 stamps in her stamp collection. Jane has

       half as many. How many stamps does Jane have?

13.   Write the number shown on the

       abacus in figures.

14.   What fraction of the circle is shown by

       the shaded area?

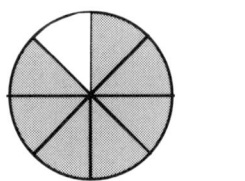

15.   Add £1.75 and 20p.

Test 37   Date........... Name...................

1.   Add 14 and 10.

2.   Find 4 lots of 9.

3.   Subtract 8 from 20.

4.   What is one hour 30 minutes later than the time shown on the clock?

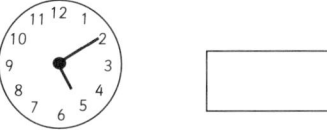

5.   I buy a can of Coke at 25p, a packet of biscuits at 75p and a chocolate bar at 10p. How much do I spend altogether?

6.   Take 50p from the answer to number 5.

7.   Double 16.

8.   Share 27 among 3.

9.   What is one more than 68?

10.   What is one less then 154?

11.   Alex was facing North. If he turned clockwise through 270° which way would he face?

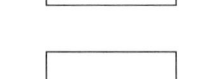

12.   [   ] - 9 = 8

13.   Multiply 275 by 10.

14.   The chart is an excerpt from a T.V. timetable. How long was the episode of Neighbours?

1.40	Neighbours
2.05	Ironside
2.55	Body Splits

15.   270 ÷ 10

Test 38   Date........... Name...................

1. Add nine to twelve.

   Answer in words.

2. From 16 take 7.

3. What is the value of 9 in 193?

4. Write the number shown on the abacus

   in figures.

Th   h   t   u

5. Decrease 17 by 4.

6. Add eighteen and nine.

7. Jane and Kate share a bar of chocolate equally. If there are 16

   squares in the bar, how many squares do they each have?

8. Take seven from a hundred and twenty.

9. Share 8 oranges among 4 children. How many each?

10. Add ten to 100.

11. 246 x 10 =

12. 8km is 5 miles. How many kilometres

    in 25 miles?

13. Hazel bought an exercise book for 18p. How many

    exercise books could she buy for £1.80?

14. 5 + [   ] + 3 = 15

15. The chart shows part of a train timetable.

    How long does it take to get from London

    to Berkhamsted?

London	09.00
Harrow	09.20
Watford	09.25
Berkhamsted	09.35

Test 39   Date........... Name....................

1. What is the total of 3 and 6 and 2 and 5?

2. 17 - 8 =

3. Decrease 21 by 7.

4. 8 + [ ] = 14

5. 4 x [ ] = 24

6. Write 1,509 in words.

7. 4 hens laid 48 eggs. They each laid the same

    number of eggs. How many did each hen lay?

8. What is half of 20?

9. Add ten to 99.

10. Take 5 away from 15.

11. How many right angles in 270°?

12. Increase 3,444 by 100.

13. What is the product of 9 and 8?

14. What fraction of the circle

    is shaded?

15. Which item on the shopping list is the

    | Hat | £26.40 |
    | Scarf | £6.80 |
    | Dress | £106.00 |

    most expensive?

Test 40   Date...........   Name.....................

1.   What is the sum of 4 and 6 and 9?

2.   6 + 3 + 2 + 4 =

3.   Alex is facing N.E. He turns clockwise

      through 180°, which way will he face?

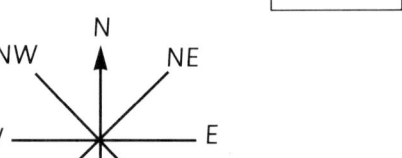

4.   4 x 8 =

5.   16 = (7 + 3) + ☐

6.   7 x 8 =

7.   Take 4 from 20.

8.   Write 717 in words.

9.   What are 6 lots of 7?

10.   Take 10 away from 48.

11.   15 - [ ] = 8

12.   Start at 7:30 finish at

      How much time has passed?

13.   Which is larger $\frac{2}{3}$ or $\frac{2}{5}$?

14.   What is the next number in the pattern? 1024, 1025, 1026

15.   £4.28 - £2.16 =

Test 41   Date........... Name......................

1. Add together 8, 4 and 3.

2. Two books cost 24p. How much is one book?

3. What is four times ten?

4. £1.12 + 8p =

5. How many tens are there in 50?

6. Which two numbers add up to 14?

   7, 8, 3, 10, 6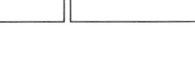

7. Eight children share 72 sweets.

   How many do each of them have?

8. 9 + [   ] = 20

9. 15 - 6 =

10. Add 10 to 1,000.

11. The shaded area is 12 cms².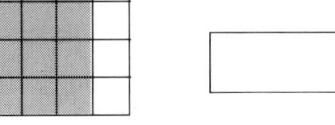

    What is the area of the shape in total?

12. What is the difference between 48 and 24?

13. What is the name of this shape?

    Tick the right box.

    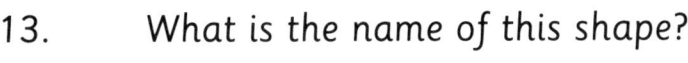
    | hexagon | octagon | pentagon | triangle |

14. What is the value of the 6 in 6,740?

15. What is the next multiple of 9?   18, 27, 36, ...

Test 42   Date.......... Name.....................

1.   What is the sum of 12 grams and 9 grams?   [   ]

2.   Take 7 from 8.   [   ]

3.   Write 1,082 in words.   [   ]

4.   5 x [   ] = 60   [   ]

5.   A man had 21 puppies and he sold 6. How many were left?   [   ]

6.   Rewrite, putting the smallest number first:-

126, 42, 29, 53, 60   [   ] [   ] [   ] [   ] [   ]

7.   How many tens in 80?   [   ]

8.   Add together £1.50, 7p and 3p.   [   ]

9.   3 + [   ] + 6 = 13   [   ]

10.   Take 4 from 46.   [   ]

11.   Show 5,065 in dots

on the abacus.

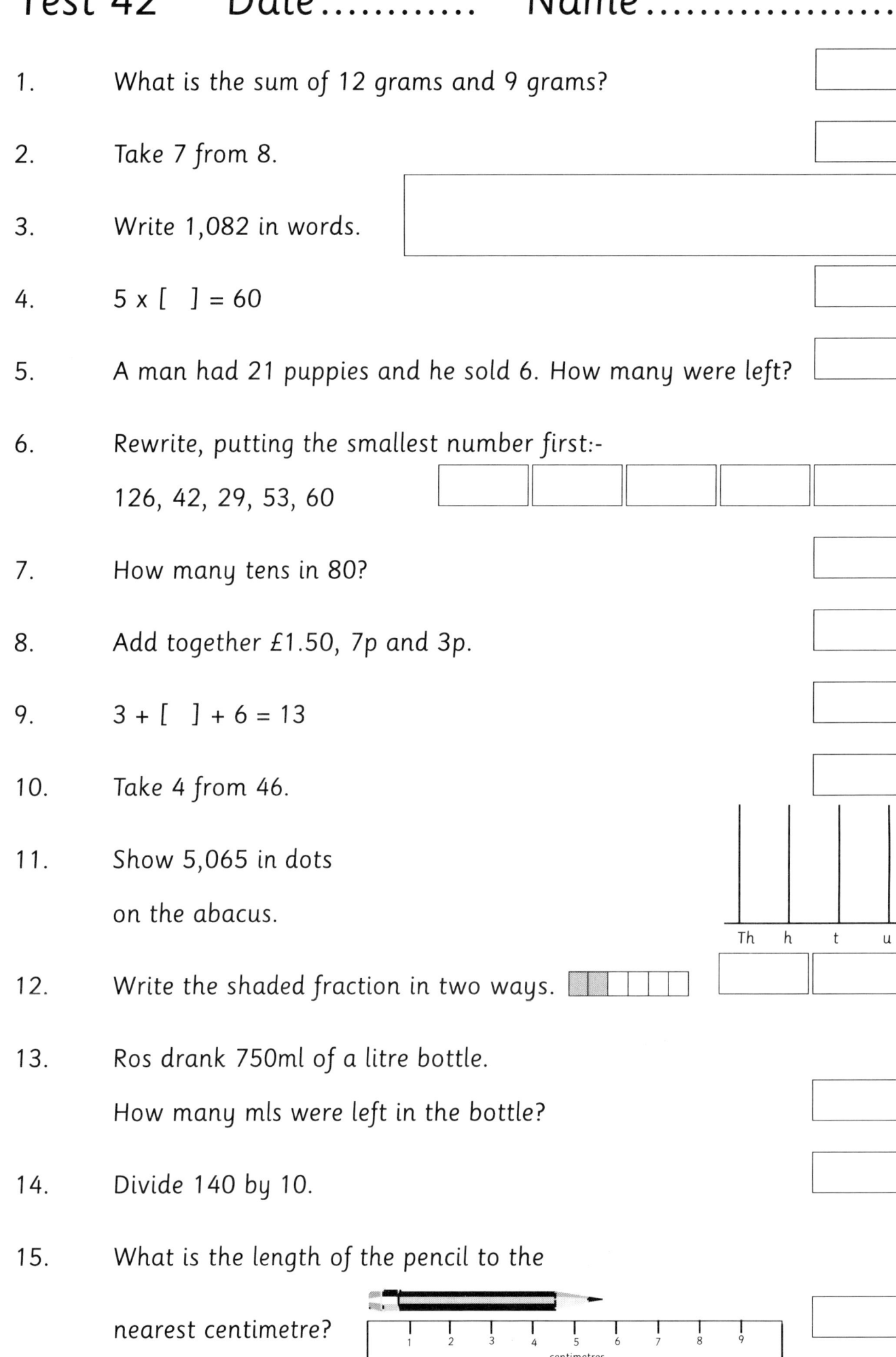

Th   h   t   u

12.   Write the shaded fraction in two ways.   [   ] [   ]

13.   Ros drank 750ml of a litre bottle.

How many mls were left in the bottle?   [   ]

14.   Divide 140 by 10.   [   ]

15.   What is the length of the pencil to the

nearest centimetre?   [   ]

centimetres

Test 43   Date.......... Name...................

1. Add one hundred and nine to ten.

   Write your answer in words. [   ]

2. Take 2 from 18. [   ]

3. Write one hundred and one in numbers. [   ]

4. Multiply 6 by 6. [   ]

5. 9 = [   ] + 4 [   ]

6. 14 - 10 = [   ]

7. Write 4,376 in words. [   ]

8. Add three to one hundred and twenty-seven. [   ]

9. Take 4 away from 30. [   ]

10. Take 10 away from 68. [   ]

11. $(1 + {}^3/_4) + \boxed{} = 2{}^1/_4$ [   ]

12. Start at 8.15pm and finish at 1:30am. How much

    time has passed? [   ]

13. Write the number shown

    on the abacus.

    Th   h   t   u [   ]

14. 4kgs of apples were bought at 25p per kilo.

    How much money was spent? [   ]

15. Double 25 and add 3. [   ]

Test 44   Date...........   Name.....................

1. What is the total of 90, 8 and 3?

2. Fred caught 7 fish, Jim caught 8 and

   Joe caught 6. What is the total?

3. Three people each won five Mars bars in a competition.

   How many Mars bars altogether?

4. Put these numbers in order smallest first:-

   2917, 1927, 9172, 1729

5. 8 + 3 + [ ] = 14

6. 17 - [ ] = 9

7. What is half of 18?

8. Claire had £1.25. She spent 8p. What was left?

9. Add 10 to 58.

10. Write one hundred and fourteen in figures.

11. Tick the name

    of the shape. | triangle | hexagon | octagon | pentagon |

12. 18 - 11 =

13. What is $^1/_{10}$ of 30?

14. Treble 9 and then add 4.

15. Start at [7:30] finish at (clock).

    How much time has passed?

Test 45   Date........... Name..................

1. What is the total of 8, 7 and 3?

2. Take 6 from 16.

3. What is $^1/_2$ of 12?

4. Take 3 away from the smallest number.   14, 16, 9, 21, 10

5. Multiply 8 by 4.

6. What is the value of 4 in 246?

7. Take two from sixty-two.

    Answer in words.

8. 6 x 6 =

9. 19 - 7 =

10. Write one thousand, one hundred and twenty-seven

    in numbers

11. The radius of a circle is 25cms. What is its diameter?

12. What fraction of the shoes

    is within the ring?

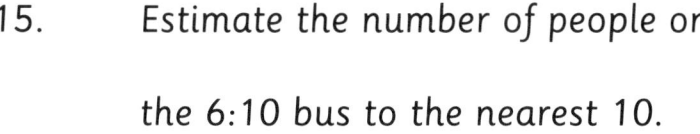

13. In a test John scored 10, Kate scored 15 and Sarah

    scored 11. What was their average score?

14. How much time passed between the

    first and last buses?

15. Estimate the number of people on

    the 6:10 bus to the nearest 10.

Test 46   Date........... Name.....................

1. Find the sum of 146 and 6.

2. What is 8 less than 19?

3. Take 30p from £1.90.

4. Take the smallest number from the largest:-

    8, 10, 3, 15, 7

5. Multiply 12 by 7.

6. I have £1.20 to spend. I buy a cake for 15p.

    What change do I have?

7. Write 2,675 in words.
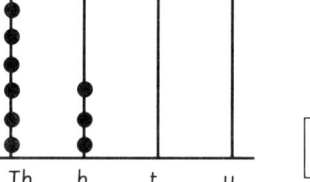

8. What is half of 1,000 chocolate biscuits?

9. $(9 + 1 + 5 + 2) + \boxed{} = 20$

10. $\boxed{} + (1 + 5) = 10$

11. Write the number shown

    on the abacus in figures.

    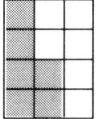
    Th   h   t   u

12. What is the value of the 9 in 6,976?

13. $(30 - 3) \div 3 =$

14. Write as a fraction the shaded part of this shape

    in 2 different ways.

15. What is 1,365 pence written as pounds and pence?

Test 47   Date........... Name........................

1.   Add together 6 and 7 and 5.

2.   Take 8 from 12.

3.   3 x 9 =

4.   Add 19p to £1.80.

5.   7 + [ ] = 12

6.   Share 10 sweets between 5 girls. How many each?

7.   Write two thousand four hundred and forty-three in figures.

8.   2 x [ ] = 18

9.   Which is the largest number?

      147, 86, 122, 61, 212

10.   What is two more than 18?

11.   What is the area of this rectangle

      in square centimetres?

12.   50 = (6 x ☐) + 2

13.   How many lines of symmetry could you draw

      on this isosceles triangle?

14.   £2.60 + £6.26

15.   Write the number shown on the

      abacus in figures.

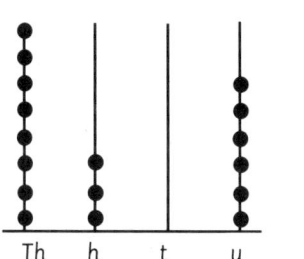

Th   h   t   u

Test 48   Date............   Name....................

1. Add together 8, 4 and 5.

2. Subtract 6 from 10.

3. What are 7 lots of 8?

4. $12 - [\quad] = 4$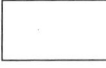

5. What is the value of 3 in 3,472?

6. $[\quad] + 5 + 4 = 12$

7. Write 674 in words.

8. $4 \times 6 =$

9. Take 4 away from 30.

10. Take 10 away from 68.

11. Show 6,312 by drawing dots on the abacus.

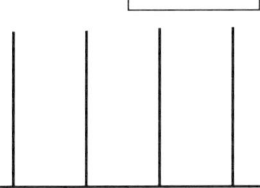

12. $46 = (6 \times \boxed{\quad}) + 4$

13. Alex faces N.W. If he turns clockwise through 90° which way will he face?

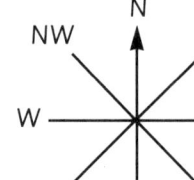

14. $9,106 - 100 =$

15. The chart shows part of a snooker scoreboard. The arrows show the scores of players 1 and 2. How much more did Player 2 score than Player 1?

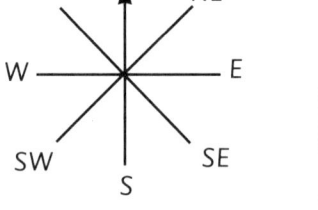

Test 49   Date............   Name........................

1. What is 5 + 14 + 1?

2. Take 7 from 21.

3. Share 32 among 8.

4. Multiply 9 by 12.

5. What is $\frac{1}{4}$ of 36?

6. 3 + [   ] = 11

7. What is the value of 9 in 9,210?

8. What are 10 lots of 33?

9. Write 2,435 in words.

10. Add ten to 101.

11. Write the number shown on the

    abacus in figures.

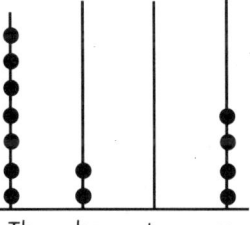
Th   h   t   u

12. What is $\frac{1}{5}$ of 35?

13. Write the number indicated by the dot

    as a decimal number.

14. Write the answer to number 13 as a mixed number fraction.

15. 50 = (8 x [   ]) + 2

Test 50   Date........... Name.....................

1.   Find the total of 7, 8 and 4.   ☐

2.   Put these in order, smallest first:-   ☐ ☐ ☐ ☐
      1340, 1350, 1450, 1230

3.   9 x 9 =   ☐

4.   Share 30 into 3 groups.   ☐

5.   What are six lots of five?   ☐

6.   Write the number indicated by the dot as a
      decimal number.   8   ● 9   ☐

7.   Write the answer to number 6 as a mixed number fraction.   ☐

8.   16 = 20 - [   ]   ☐

9.   Take 3 from 36.   ☐

10.   18 - 3 =   ☐

11.   What is 10 more than 55?   ☐

12.   Share 150 among 10.   ☐

13.   Write the number shown on the abacus   ☐
                                              Th   h   t   u

14.   Kate bought items costing £1.63 and £6.27.   ☐
      How much did she spend?

15.   The chart shows part of a train timetable.

London	09:06
Darlington	13:20
Edinburgh	18:30

      How long does it take to get from London to Edinburgh?   ☐

Test 51   Date............   Name....................

1. What is the sum of 10 and 12?

2. Take 8 from 48.

3. Alex faces S.W. If he turns clockwise

   through 270° where will he then face?

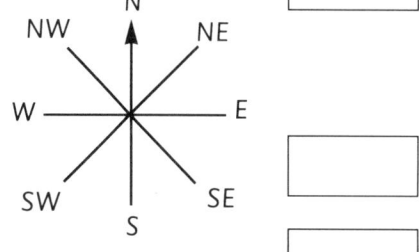

4. I spend 48p out of £1.00. How much is left?

5. Share 35p among 5 children.

   How much each?

6. How many millilitres are in the jug?

7. Share 120 among 10.

8. 106 + 4 = [   ]

9. Take 10 from 110.

10. 25 x 10

11. 8 x 7 =

12. Write the number indicated by the dot

    as a decimal number.

13. Write the answer to number 12 as a mixed number fraction.

14. What is $\frac{1}{3}$ of 33p?

15. Write the number shown on the

    abacus as a decimal number.

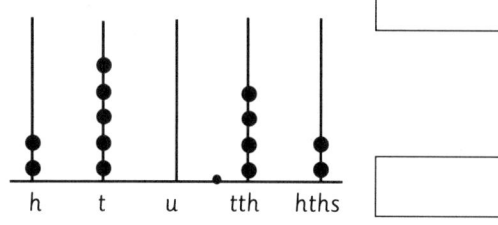

Test 52   Date........... Name....................

1. What is the value of 9 in 1,395?

2. What is $^1/_4$ of 16?

3. What fraction of the faces are within the star?

4. Write the answer to number 3 as a decimal fraction.

5. Divide 81 by 9.

6. Multiply 6 by 7.

7. Which is the largest amount?

   £3.48, £3.87 or £3.78?

8. Add together £1.23 and 7p.

9. If a piece of chocolate weighs 8 grams what do 10 pieces of chocolate weigh?

10. 7 + 5 = 20 - [   ]

11. How many metres from point A to D?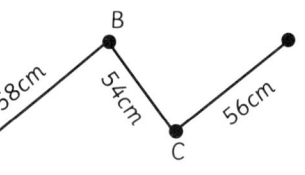

    Write your answer as a decimal number.

12. What is $^3/_4$ of 16?

13. Add 4, 5 and 8.

14. Write the number shown on the abacus as a decimal number.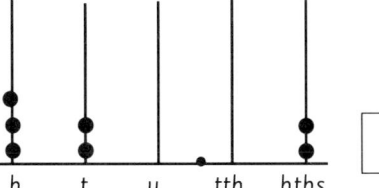

15. What time is two and a half hours before 10:30pm?

Test 53   Date........... Name........................

1. Add 7 to 19.

2. Which two of these numbers add up to 15?

    4, 8, 6, 7, 3

3. What are 6 lots of 12?

4. Share 36 cakes among 6 boys. How many for each boy?

5. What are 8 cakes at 6p each?

6. Take 11 from 28.

7. Share 320 among 10.

8. Put in order, largest amount first:-

    95p, £1.20, 67p, £3.68

9. What is the value of 2 in 342?

10. What is $^1/_5$ of 25?

11. Express the shaded fraction of the

    circle as a decimal.

12. 65 = (8 x ☐) + 1

13. How long is the pencil?

    Answer as a decimal number.

14. Each line is half as long as the one above.

    How long is the shortest line?

15. $^3/_4$ of 1 metre = [   ]cms

Test 54   Date...........   Name.....................

1.   Add together 14 and 7 and 2.

2.   19 - 9 =

3.   Start at 9:45am finish at  pm.

   How much time has passed in hours and minutes?

4.   Share 35 by 5.

5.   Add 15p, 8p and 3p.

6.   How many tens in 190?

7.   Write 2,256 in words.

8.   Add 10 to the largest number:-   74, 32, 14, 81, 78.

9.   2 + [   ] + 4 = 12

10.   Take one from 6 x 3.

11.   Write the decimal number shown

   on the abacus in figures.

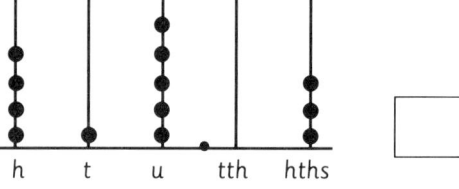

12. $^1/_3$ of 1 hour = [   ]minutes

13.   How much change would Jo get from £5 if she

   bought an item costing £3.64?

14.   Estimate the whole number as marked

   by the arrow on the line.

15.   Multiply 6 by 7.

Test 55   Date.......... Name.................

1. What is the total of 17 and 6?

2. What is five less than eighteen?

    Answer in words.

3. Penny had £1.20 and spent 12p.

    How much does she have left?

4. What is 72 shared among 12?

5. A pencil is 12cm long. How many metres

    would 12 pencils be? Answer as a decimal number.

6. How many tens in 190?

7. Multiply 17 by 10.

8. Add 10cms to 2 lots of 5cms.

9. Write 2,783 in words.

10. What is 100 less than 1000?

11. Write the weight in kgs shown on the

    scale as a decimal.

12. How many minutes in $\frac{2}{3}$ of 1 hour?

13. Draw dots to show 56.05 on the abacus.

    h   t   u   tth   hths

14. If ● represents 2 children, look at the diagram

    to see how many children walked to school.

    car ●●◖
    bus ●
    walk ●●●●●◖
    bike ●●●

15. If there are 24 children in the class what

    fraction went by bike to school?

Test 56   Date........... Name.....................

1. How many corners does a rectangle have? □

2. What is the next number?   0, 6, 12, 18, 12, 6 □

3. What time is ten minutes after twenty past three? □

4. Which day is two days before Wednesday? □

5. Seven children ate 4 sandwiches each.

   How many sandwiches were eaten? □

6. An apple costs 8p. How much for 9 apples? □

7. Write 2 numbers which add up to 10 □ □

8. What is $^1/_3$ of 24? □

9. How many quarters are there in a whole? □

10. Add 2 to 109. □

11. If the jar when full holds 1000 sweets,

    estimate how many are left. □

12. What is $^3/_4$ written as a decimal? □

13. A van went East for 600m, South for

    600 metres   400 m   1600 metres

    400m then East for 1600 m.

    How many kms? Answer as a decimal. □

14. The distance from Penzance to Leeds is 375 miles.

    Round this distance to the nearest 100 miles. □

15. If 9 pears cost 86p what change would be given

    from a £2 coin? □

Test 57   Date.......... Name...................

1.   How many corners has a circle?

2.   What is the next number?   7, 14, 21

3.   Is 567 an even number?

4.   Jenny lived for a decade. How old was she?

5.   There are 12 bottles in a crate.

      How many bottles are there in 7 crates?

6.   (20p + 20p) + ☐ = 50p

7.   Which month comes before October?

8.   A cake costs 9p. How much do a dozen cakes cost?

9.   Estimate the position of the
      arrow on the line.

10.   How many times does 6 fit into 54?

11.   48 ÷ 8 =

12.   Write the number shown on the
      abacus as a decimal.

13.   How many times larger is 250 than 25?

14.   Divide 9,000 by 10.

15.   Write the weight in kilograms as shown by the
      arrow. Write your answer as a decimal number.
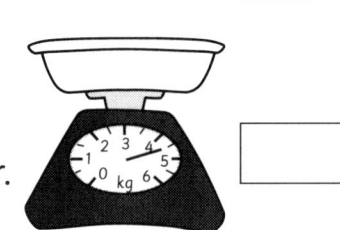

Test 58   Date........... Name.....................

1. How many days are there in 3 weeks?

2. Jennifer's bean grew 7cms. The next week it grew 11cms.

   What does it measure now?

3. $(5p + 5p) + \boxed{} = 15p$

4. How many centimetres is

   the pencil? Write your answer as a decimal.

5. Sally is 14 years old. How old was she 9 years ago?

6. Add these numbers:-   3, 6, 2, 9

7. What is the difference between 12 and 16?

8. Multiply these numbers:-   4, 9.

9. Divide 88 by 11.

10. Share 56 doughnuts among 7 people. How many each?

11. If there are 20 children in a class,

    what fraction of them have had

Illness	No. of children
mumps	𝍷𝍷𝍷𝍷 𝍷𝍷𝍷𝍷
flu	III
chickenpox	𝍷𝍷𝍷𝍷 II

    mumps?

12. 2 doughnuts cost 36p. How much would 10 doughnuts be?

13. $^4/_5$ of 1 min = [   ] seconds

14. What is the next number?   9, 7, 5

15. How many hours and minutes longer is 7:30

    than the time shown on the clock?

Test 59   Date........... Name.....................

1. What is the total of 4 and 15?

2. 19 - 12 =

3. Draw 508.64 as dots on

   the abacus.

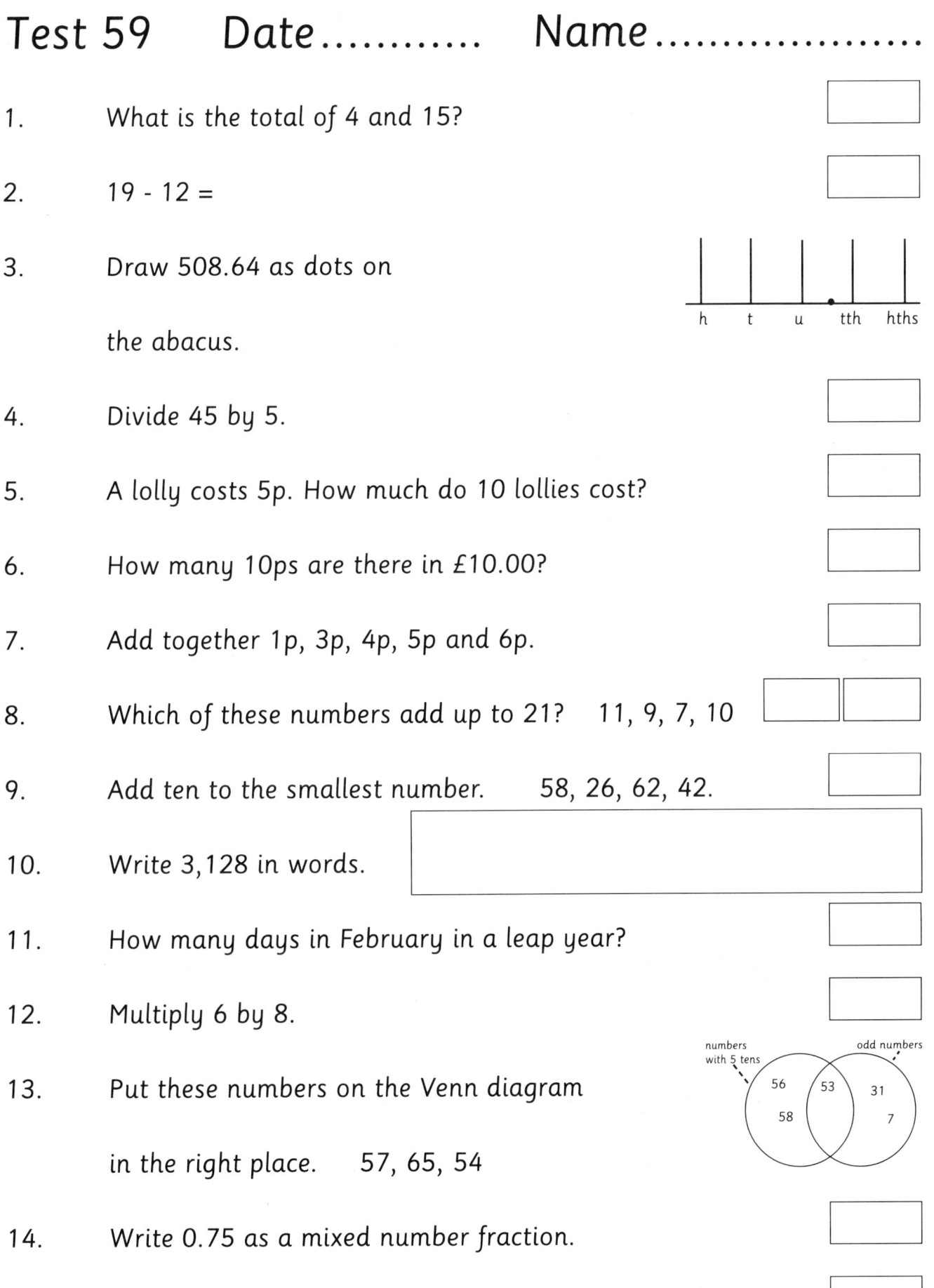

4. Divide 45 by 5.

5. A lolly costs 5p. How much do 10 lollies cost?

6. How many 10ps are there in £10.00?

7. Add together 1p, 3p, 4p, 5p and 6p.

8. Which of these numbers add up to 21?   11, 9, 7, 10

9. Add ten to the smallest number.   58, 26, 62, 42.

10. Write 3,128 in words.

11. How many days in February in a leap year?

12. Multiply 6 by 8.

13. Put these numbers on the Venn diagram

    in the right place.   57, 65, 54

14. Write 0.75 as a mixed number fraction.

15. What is $\frac{1}{5}$ of £15?

Test 60   Date........... Name...................

1.   What is the sum of 8 and 15?

2.   Nick got on the bus at 8:15am. His journey took until
        the time shown on the clock.
        How long was his journey?

3.   Multiply 6 by 5.

4.   How much change will I get from £6.20p if I spend £1.13p?

5. $(12 + 7) +$ ☐ $= 25$

6.   What are 10 lots of 36p?

7.   Take 10 away from the largest number.   129, 16, 138, 119

8.   How many minutes are there in 1 hour 2 minutes?

9.   How many tens are there in 170?

10.   What is the value of 3 in 123?

11.   From 17 take 13.

12.   How many litres altogether are shown
        in both jugs? Answer as a decimal number.

13.   What is $^1/_4$ of 30cms? Answer as a decimal.

14.   Write the number shown on the
        abacus as a decimal.

15.   Write the shaded parts as
        a mixed number fraction.

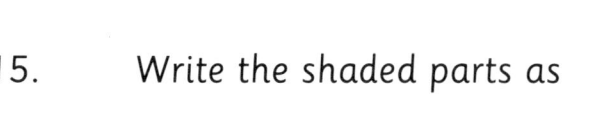
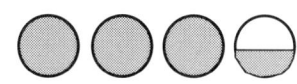

Test 61   Date........... Name...................

1.   Add 19 and 7.

2.   Add $^1/_2$ of 12 to $^1/_4$ of 12.

3.   From 23 take 6.

4.   What is $^1/_3$ of 18?

5.   What time is a quarter of an hour past two o'clock in the

        afternoon? Write this digitally as for a 24 hour clock.

6.   Multiply 12 by 8.

7.   Share 15 by 5.

8.   21 - 7 =

9.   Share 36 sweets among 4 groups.

10.   What time is ten minutes later than 8:20am?

11.   Round 6.7m to the nearest metre.

12.   Write the number shown on the

        chart as a decimal.

13.   What would the answer to number 12 be as a fraction?

14.   Add 6, $^3/_4$ and $^1/_2$ together.

15.   What fraction of the men

        is ringed?

Test 62   Date........... Name.........................

1. Give all 24 in the class 2 sweets each.

    How many sweets would you need?   [ ]

2. Add 16 and 8 and 5.   [ ]

3. Take 8 from 20.   [ ]

4. Multiply 19 by 10.   [ ]

5. Add 10 to the answer to number 4.   [ ]

6. What do I have to add to 8 to give an answer of 14?   [ ]

7. Divide 18 by 6.   [ ]

8. There are 7 tables at a lunch. Each table holds 12 people.

    How many people will the tables hold altogether?   [ ]

9. Add 9, 3, 2 and 6 together.   [ ]

10. What is the shape shown called?   [ ]

11. A pair of shoes cost £11. How much would eight pairs cost? [ ]

12. Write three-hundredths as a decimal.   [ ]

13. Write the number shown on the

    abacus as a decimal.   [ ]
                               h   t   u   tth   hths

14. How much time will pass between pm

    and [14:00] ?   [ ]

15. 2.3 x 10 =   [ ]

Test 63   Date............   Name.........................

1.   How many legs do seven spiders have?   ☐

2.   Fluffy the cat has five kittens. How many ears
      and tails do the kittens have altogether?   ☐

3.   What is one hundred and thirteen take away nine?
      Answer in words.   ☐

4.   5 + 10 + 5 =   ☐

5.   What is the value of 6 in 6,059?   ☐

6.   What is a quarter of 16?   ☐

7.   What is $^1/_3$ of 27?   ☐

8.   The 🐦 represents 5 birds
      coming to visit the bird table.

      | Blue tits | 🐦 🐦 🐦 🐦 🐦 🐦 |
      | Sparrows | 🐦 🐦 🐦 🐦 |
      | Robins | 🐦 🐦 |

      How many more blue tits than robins came to the table?   ☐

9.   What is the value of the 6 in 3,681?   ☐

10.   4 x 7 = 30 - [   ]   ☐

11.   Multiply 12 by 12.   ☐

12.   Write the length of the pencil
      in centimetres. Answer as a decimal number.   ☐

13.   A dress costing £62.58 was reduced to half price in the sale.
      How much did it cost?   ☐

14.   What is the weight in kilograms shown
      on the scales? Answer as a decimal.   ☐

15.   How many grams are there in $^1/_2$ kilogram?   ☐

Test 64   Date...........   Name.....................

1.   Multiply 6 by 7 then add 4.

2.   Add 12 and 8, then take away 5.

3. $48 \div 12 =$

4.   How many legs do 8 dogs have?

5.   You buy a chocolate bar costing 10p, a cake

   costing 15p and a pie costing £1.06. How much do you

   spend altogether?

6.   What is $^1/_2$ of 24?

7.   Add $^1/_2$ of 10 to $^1/_4$ of 8?

8.   What is $^1/_6$ of 24?

9.   Share 28 books among 7 people.

10.   Alex is facing S.E. If he turns anti-clockwise

   through 270°, which way would he face?

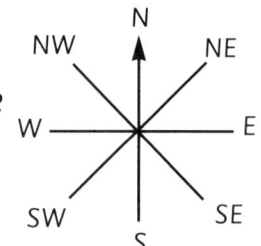

11.   Subtract 11 from 19.

12.   Is 57 a multiple of 3?

13.   Draw the dots on the abacus

   to show 207.45.

   h   t   u   tth   hths

14.   Sue completed 4 out of 12 tests. What fraction

   of the tests did she still have to complete?

15.   Adam rode his bike North for 300m,

   East for 250m, South for 100m and East for 550m.

   How far did he travel in kilometres? Answer as a decimal.

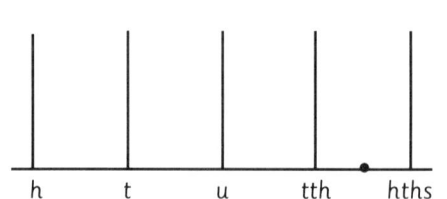

Test 65   Date........... Name...................

1.   Add nine to two hundred and twenty-one. Answer in figures.

2.   4 x 8 = [   ] - 8

3.   I have 64p to spend on flowers. Each flower costs 8p.

      How many can I buy?

4.   What is the area of the square

      in square centimetres?

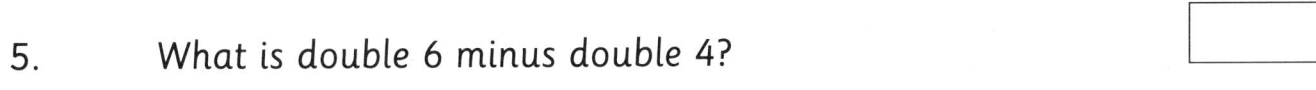
4cms

4cms

5.   What is double 6 minus double 4?

6.   From 19 take 7.

7.   What is $^1/_6$ of 54?

8.   What time is it 3 hours after the time

      shown on the clock?

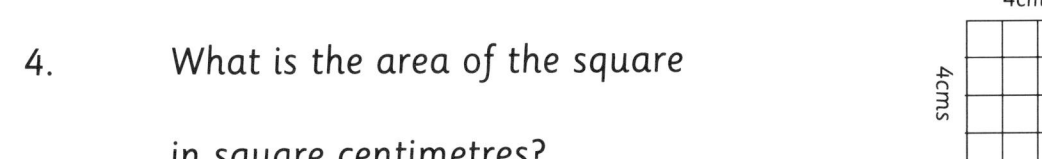

9.   What is the value of the 8 in 8,397?

10.   6 x 6 = [   ] - 8

11.   The chart shows how many fish a whale

      ate in 3 days. How many fish did the

      whale eat altogether?

No. of fish
50
30
10
1st 2nd 3rd
days

12.   Write 0.75 as a fraction.

13.   What are four lots of seven?

14.   How many degrees of angle in a semi-circle?

15.   What is the number shown on the

      abacus as a decimal?

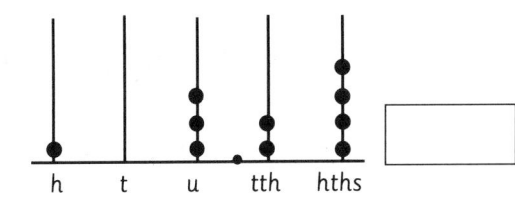
h   t   u   tth   hths

Test 66   Date...........   Name...................

1. Add together 14 and 7 and 2.

2. 119 - 9 =

3. Multiply 6 by 7.

4. Share 45 by 5.

5. Add 15p, 8p and 3p.

6. How many tens in 190?

7. Write 2,256 in words.

8. Add 10 to the largest number.   74, 32, 14, 81, 78.

9. 2 + [   ] + 4 = 12

10. Take one from 6 x 3.

11. The diagram shows part of a thermometer.
    What is the temperature in °C?

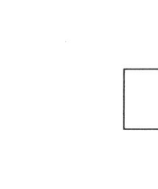

12. What is the difference in °C of
    temperature between the answer to number 11
    and the hottest part of the day which was 10°C?

13. What is the perimeter in metres of
    this triangle? Answer in a decimal number.

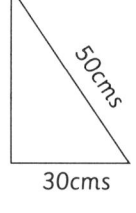

40cms   50cms   30cms

14. 12 shirts cost £144. How much did one shirt cost?

15. John started his journey at  am and stopped at 15:30
    How long had he been travelling?

Test 67   Date............   Name....................

1. Write nine thousand, seven hundred and four in numbers. □

2. Divide twenty-eight by seven. □

3. 25 ÷ [   ] = 5 □

4. A pencil case holds five pencils. How many pencils
    will eight pencil cases hold? □

5. Add 6, 7, 4, 1 and 2. □

6. What is a third of 36? □

7. Mrs P buys six bars of chocolate to do chocolate
    fractions with Year 4. If each bar has twelve squares
    of chocolate, how many squares are there altogether? □

8. What is the value of 9 in 5,894? □

9. [   ] x 6 = 42 □

10. Share 35 among 4. What is the remainder? □ r □

11. Write the number shown by the
    arrow as a decimal. □

12. The diagram shows part of a thermometer.
    What is the temperature in °C?---------------------- □

13. Is 5 a prime number? □

14. Add £5.60 and £2.23 □

15. Use the number line
    to help work out -9 + 6 □

Test 68   Date........... Name.....................

1.   9 + 4 = [   ] + 3

2.   What time is a quarter of an hour before three thirty?

3.   Add 12p, 8p and 5p.

4.   Add £1.55 and £3.45.

5.   Divide thirty-four by six. What is the answer

and what is the remainder?   r

6.   Subtract 7 from 16.

7.   18 - [   ] = 7

8.   Write 7,605 in words.

9.   5 x 7 = [   ] - 5

10.   Add four, twelve and five.

11.   Use the number line to help work

out -7 + 12.

12.   The diagram shows part of a thermometer.

What is the temperature in °C?

13.   What are the 5 prime numbers

between 0 and 10?

14.   Add 45 centimetres to 3 metres.

Write your answer as a decimal.

15.   How many litres are shown altogether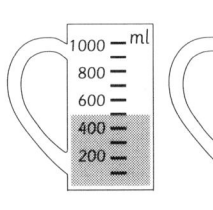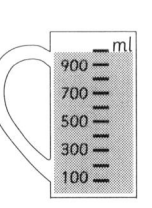

in both jugs? Answer as a decimal.

Test 69   Date........... Name...................

1. How many egg boxes will you need for 24 eggs,

    if each egg box holds 6 eggs?

2. Divide 37 by 6. What is the answer and

    what is the remainder?   r

3. 5 x 12 =

4. 4 x 8 =

5. 7 + 4 = [ ] - 14

6. (8 x 7) - 6 =

7. What is $^1/_2$ of 22?

8. Double 9 then add 4.

9. 7 + 3 = 9 + [ ]

10. Double [ ] + 1 = 19

11. If each wine carafe holds a litre, estimate
    how many litres of wine there are
    altogether. Answer as a decimal.

    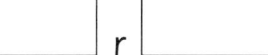

12. Use the number line to help
    work out -8 + 14.

    -10   -5   0   5   10

13. What is 13 to the nearest 10?

14. Jan bought 12 tennis balls costing 12p each. How
    much change would he receive if he paid with a £2 coin?

15. Write the number shown on the
    abacus in figures.

    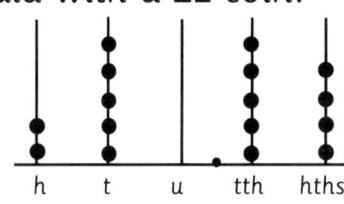

    h   t   u   tth   hths

Test 70   Date........... Name....................

1. Write 2,596 in words.

2. Write fifty-six thousand, two hundred and

    seventy-eight in numbers.

    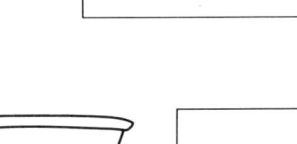

3. What is ten more than 125?

4. Write the weight shown by the arrow on the

    scales in kg. Give your answer as a decimal.

5. What is a hundred years called?

6. How many tens are there in 100?

7. Multiply eight by nine.

8. Take 10 away from 67.

9. ☐ + (8 + 9) = 25

10. 9 = [   ] - 8 - 10

11. The diagram shows part of a thermometer.

    What is the temperature in °C?

    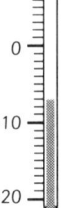

12. What are the 4 prime numbers between

    10 and 20?

    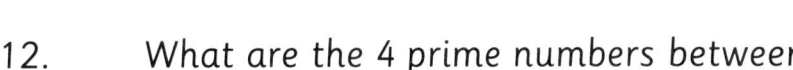

13. Use the number line to help

    work out -10 + 8.

14. Add 6p, 7p, 9p and 10p.

15. Julia bought 3 different colours of nail varnish

Test 71   Date............   Name....................

1.   Multiply 2.1 by 4.

2.   What is $\frac{1}{10}$ of 320?

3.   What is the next number?   140, 143, 146

4.   What is 9 worth in 9,486?

5.   What is the value of 6 in 7,639?

6.   Write 3 metres 46cms in metres using a decimal point.

7.   8 x 7 =

8.   Draw dots to show 56.07

    on the abacus.

9.   Multiply £5.00 by 3.

10.   How many eggs are there in 12 boxes

    if each box holds 6 eggs?

11.   What fraction of the hamburgers

    is ringed?

12.   54 ÷ 9 =

13.   Add 3.2 and 2.6

14.   If the temperature shown on the thermometer

    was to rise by 4°C, what would the temperature be?

15.   Vicky bought 4 cinema tickets for £6.30 each.

    How much did she pay?

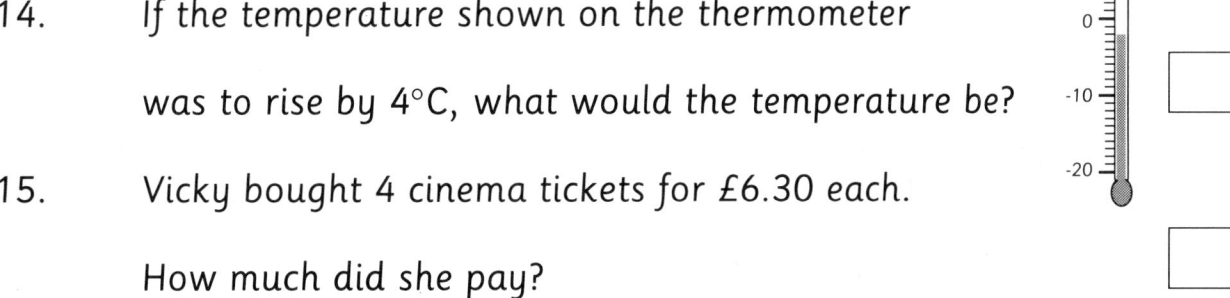

Test 72   Date.......... Name...................

1. Sixteen minus twelve equals [   ].

2. Take 10 from the largest number:-   41, 80, 96, 32, 16

3. What is the difference between 80 and 90?

4. Write 7,606 in words.

5. Which three numbers add up to 20?

   7, 3, 8, 5, 6, 2

6. A chocolate box holds 36 chocolates in 4 rows.

   How many chocolates are there in each row?

7. A man started work at 14:00 and finished

   at (clock) pm. How long did he work?

8. 8 + 9 + 5 - 8 =

9. 8 x 8 =

10. 6 x 7 = [   ] + 5

11. How much change from a £5 note would

    there be if £2.86 was spent?

12. If the temperature shown on the thermometer

    was to rise by 6°C what temperature would it be?

13. Write $6^1/_2$ grams as a decimal.

14. What is the area of the shape shown

    in square centimetres?

    4cm

    3cm

15. What is the perimeter of the shape shown?

Name ....

Graph to show the number of "right first time" answers in 'Mental Arithmetic Tests' through Year 4.

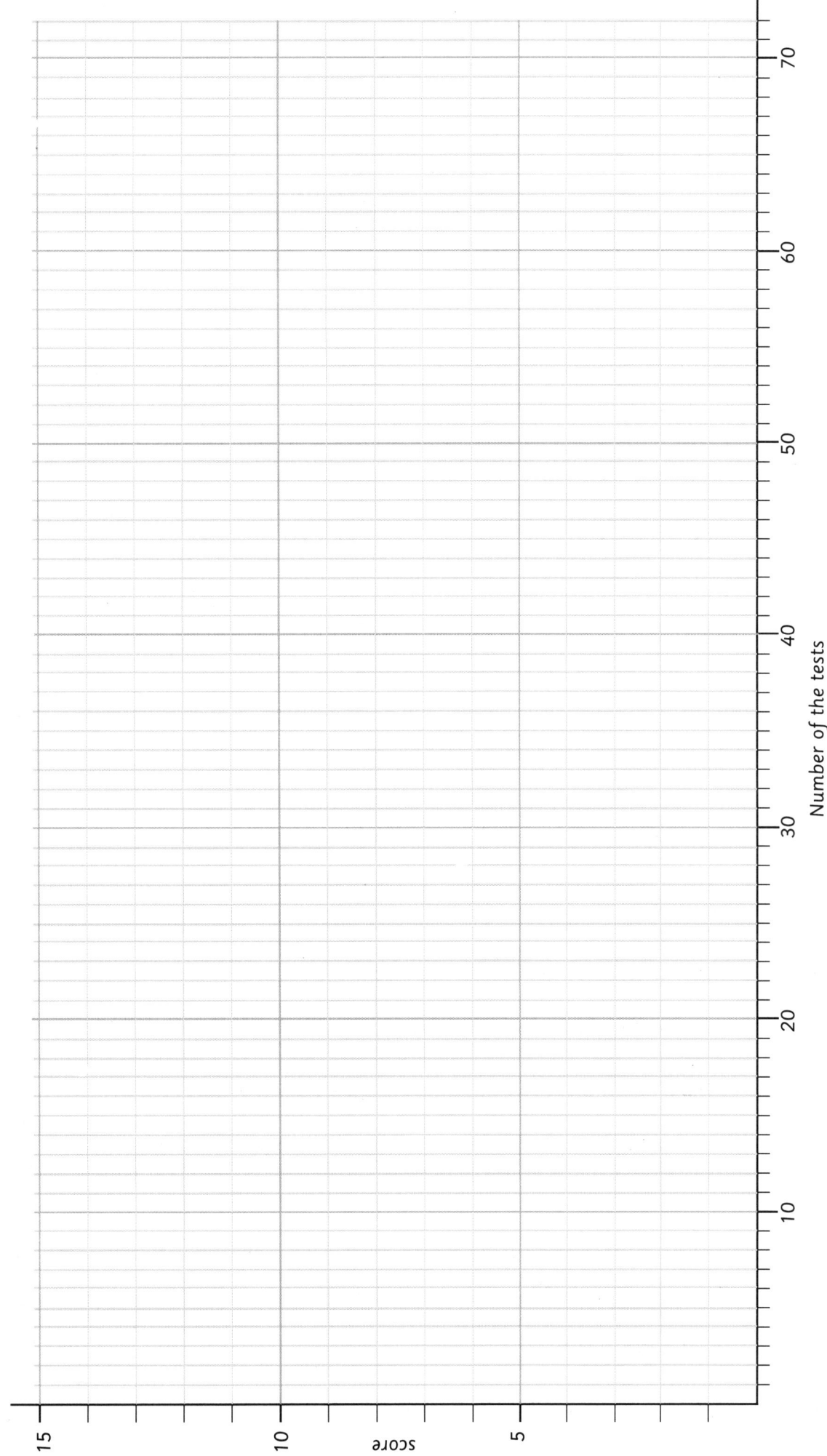

Number of the tests

score

Put a cross (✖) for each score after you finish each booklet . Draw a line to join each cross. Use a ruler to help you.

Answers Test 1

1. 12
2. 7
3. 14
4. 16
5. 6
6. 17, 19, 21
7. 7
8. 20
9. thirty-seven
10. 23
11. -----
12. 58
13. 106
14. 4 litres
15. $^3/_4$

Answers Test 2

1. 15
2. 16
3. 15
4. 12p
5. 5
6. 3
7. 35
8. 124
9. six hundred and forty
10. 29
11. 14
12. 3cm
13. 60
14. 90°
15. 26 minutes

Answers Test 3

1. 12
2. 7
3. 18
4. 4
5. 10
6. 41
7. 5
8. 226
9. 40
10. 18, 21, 36, 41
11. five hundred and seven
12. 54
13. 59
14. 8
15. -----

Answers Test 4

1. 23
2. 7
3. 45° (approx)
4. 15
5. 40
6. 6
7. 14
8. 35
9. three hundred and thirty-eight
10. 29
11. 40
12. 26
13. 72
14. 6
15. 8 litres

Answers Test 5

1. 15
2. 9
3. 5
4. 12
5. 21
6. one hundred and thirty-seven
7. 40
8. 14
9. 3
10. 161
11. £1
12. 20
13. even
14. 367
15. $^1/_4$

Answers Test 6

1. 8:05
2. 19
3. 12
4. 19p
5. 42
6. 12
7. 8
8. three hundred and thirty-nine
9. 19
10. 37
11. 27, 21, 17, 13
12. 1 hr 15 mins
13. 4
14. 6
15. £3.80

Answers Test 7

1. 18
2. 8
3. 36
4. 12
5. 7
6. two hundred and forty-eight
7. 4
8. 50
9. 39
10. 22
11. 500mls
12. 75p
13. 4:00
14. 648
15. $\frac{1}{3}$

Answers Test 8

1. 19
2. 14
3. 24
4. 8
5. 21p
6. 2
7. 126
8. 7, 3
9. 13
10. 30
11. triangle
12. 31
13. 5
14. 6
15. 3

Answers Test 9

1. 19
2. 8
3. 18
4. 17
5. 10
6. four hundred and eighty-seven
7. 24
8. 10
9. 23
10. -----
11. 18, 43, 99, 170, 213
12. 8
13. 20p
14. £1.77
15. £5.05

Answers Test 10

1. 17
2. 6
3. 6p
4. 13cm²
5. 45
6. 946
7. 312
8. 98
9. 21p
10. 17
11. 18
12. $\frac{3}{4}$
13. 32
14. £4.88
15. 4

Answers Test 11

1. 19
2. 9
3. 13
4. 1970
5. 6
6. 16
7. 5
8. 36
9. 10
10. 10, 11, 14, 16
11. ----------------
12. 16
13. 9
14. 105cms
15. $\frac{1}{3}$

Answers Test 12

1. 15
2. 7
3. 24
4. 54cm + 46cm = 1m
5. 8
6. 30
7. 44
8. one hundred and thirty-two
9. 9
10. 7
11. 15
12. 17p
13. 10
14. £1, 50p 5p
15. 360g

Answers Test 13

1. 14
2. 5
3. 20p
4. 10
5. 22p
6. 6
7. 39
8. 106
9. 103, 42, 39, 15, 6
10. 67
11. 65
12. £8.77
13. 24
14. 9:25
15. 20cms

Answers Test 14

1. 15
2. 9
3. 30
4. 16
5. 11
6. one hundred and fifty-seven
7. 11
8. 47
9. 60
10. 53
11. 16, 17
12. 45 mins
13. £6
14. 304
15. 8:15pm

Answers Test 15

1. 17
2. 11
3. 12
4. 9
5. 20p
6. 6
7. 213, 41, 25, 7
8. 26
9. 9
10. 46
11. 75p
12. 10:30
13. 9:30
14. 54
15. 5cms

Answers Test 16

1. 14
2. 8
3. 7
4. 8 litres
5. 24
6. 293
7. 15
8. forty-one
9. 10
10. 7
11. 135° (approx)
12. 611
13. 52
14. 17
15. 60 miles

Answers Test 17

1. 23
2. 11
3. 68mls
4. 48
5. 7
6. 44
7. 80
8. 6 tens or 60
9. 40
10. 53
11. 7
12. 32cms^2
13. 26
14. 12
15. 45°

Answers Test 18

1. 21
2. 9
3. 7
4. twenty-one
5. 20p
6. two thousand, one hundred and three
7. 5
8. 7
9. 3,125
10. 8, 6
11. 17
12. 56, 156, 1056, 1156
13. $^2/_5$
14. 1570
15. 8:10

Answers Test 19

1. 16
2. 24
3. 4,036
4. 500 or 5 hundreds
5. 40p
6. 10
7. 42
8. 7,6
9. 109
10. 2,669
11. 48
12. 60mls
13. 18
14. five thousand, two hundred and sixty-seven
15. £5

Answers Test 20

1. 17 metres
2. 14
3. 3
4. 16
5. 20
6. 9
7. 2, 13, 47, 98, 120
8. 3 or 3 units
9. three hundred and sixty-seven
10. 11
11. £14.20
12. 270°
13. 90°
14. 1,177
15. 9:40

Answers Test 21

1. 24p
2. 27
3. 14
4. 20
5. 4 litres
6. 99
7. 24
8. 6
9. three thousand, five hundred and eighty-four
10. 33
11. 6,610
12. 2,502
13. 12
14. 27
15. $^1/_3$

Answers Test 22

1. 19
2. 75p
3. 5p
4. 170
5. 28
6. 20p
7. 50p
8. three thousand two hundred and ninety-two
9. 3
10. 900 or 9 hundreds
11. 15km
12. 7
13. 3,421
14. 4kg
15. 6 cms

Answers Test 23

1. 17
2. 11
3. 8p
4. 21
5. 700 or 7 hundreds
6. 1
7. 69
8. 48
9. 27p
10. 2,173
11. 310
12. 120cm or 1.20m
13. $^6/_{10}$ or $^3/_5$
14. 12:15pm
15. 340g

Answers Test 24

1. eighteen
2. 9
3. - - - - -
4. 3
5. 4
6. 20p
7. 10
8. 99
9. five hundred and thirty-eight
10. 9 or 9 units
11. 70 years
12. 5,021
13. 24
14. £6.30
15. 750g

Answers Test 25

1. 18
2. 9
3. 3hrs 15mins
4. 16
5. 56
6. one thousand, two hundred and thirty-six
7. 40
8. 29
9. 3
10. 13
11. 5
12. 166
13. 2403
14. £4.40
15. 8,631

Answers Test 26

1. 18
2. -----
3. 19p
4. 30
5. 6
6. 119
7. four hundred and fifty-two
8. 331, 231, 25, 21, 17, 3
9. 64
10. 37
11. 3
12. ------
13. 400 or 4 hundreds
14. 360°
15. 16

Answers Test 27

1. 21
2. 7
3. 72
4. 5
5. 16
6. ------
7. 9
8. seven hundred and twenty-six
9. 24
10. 7, 12, 41, 49, 111
11. 54
12. 5km
13. 9
14. 72p
15. 10

Answers Test 28

1. 19
2. 6
3. 15
4. 9:30
5. 9
6. 12
7. 11
8. one thousand eight hundred and ninety-eight
9. 440
10. 29
11. 63
12. 5,132
13. 678
14. £23.50
15. 56cm

Answers Test 29

1. 17
2. 11
3. ------
4. 18
5. 4
6. 8
7. 4
8. 18
9. seventy-four
10. 120
11. 12
12. 3
13. 36
14. £3.09
15. 420g

Answers Test 30

1. 18
2. 16
3. 30
4. W
5. 5
6. 14
7. 35
8. 69
9. 11
10. 1,146
11. 26km
12. 1,463
13. £1.12
14. 3
15. 1,310

Answers Test 31

1. 21
2. W
3. 18
4. 48
5. 6
6. 4, 7, 16, 128, 132, 1344
7. 12
8. 5
9. 36
10. 7
11. 8:55am
12. 13m
13. £3.50
14. 9
15. 3,862

Answers Test 32

1. 16
2. 7
3. - - - - - -
4. £2.18
5. 36
6. five thousand, three hundred and eighty
7. 6
8. 7
9. 24
10. 2,070
11. 4:30
12. 8
13. 90
14. N
15. 2,556

Answers Test 33

1. 22
2. 8
3. 54
4. £1.15
5. 7
6. three thousand, two hundred and eighteen
7. 19
8. 44
9. 8
10. 4102
11. 667
12. 12:20pm
13. 125
14. 2,000
15. 440g

Answers Test 34

1. 22
2. 16
3. - - - - -
4. 18
5. 19p
6. 446
7. 242
8. 1326
9. 7
10. 17p
11. 6
12. 16l
13. 3,785
14. 28
15. 8

Answers Test 35

1. 15
2. 5
3. 84
4. 27
5. 11
6. two thousand and eighty-five
7. 4
8. 50
9. 239
10. one hundred and twenty-two
11. 7:15pm
12. 750g
13. 7
14. 2,860
15. 22

Answers Test 36

1. 23
2. 15
3. 32
4. 8
5. 21p
6. 4
7. 20
8. 7, 3
9. 14
10. 40
11. 36cms
12. 36
13. 4,103
14. $^{7}/_{8}$
15. £1.95

Answers Test 37

1. 24
2. 36
3. 12
4. 6:40
5. £1.10
6. 60p
7. 32
8. 9
9. 69
10. 153
11. W
12. 17
13. 2,750
14. 25mins
15. 27

Answers Test 38

1. twenty-one
2. 9
3. 90 or 9 tens
4. 5,203
5. 13
6. 27
7. 8
8. 113
9. 2
10. 110
11. 2,460
12. 40km
13. 10
14. 7
15. 35mins

Answers Test 39

1. 16
2. 9
3. 14
4. 6
5. 6
6. one thousand, five hundred and nine
7. 12
8. 10
9. 109
10. 10
11. 3
12. 3544
13. 72
14. $^3/_8$
15. dress at £106.00

Answers Test 40

1. 19
2. 15
3. S.W.
4. 32
5. 6
6. 56
7. 16
8. seven hundred and seventeen
9. 42
10. 38
11. 7
12. 2hrs 40mins
13. $^2/_3$
14. 1027
15. £2.12

Answers Test 41

1. 15
2. 12p
3. 40
4. £1.20
5. 5
6. 8, 6
7. 9
8. 11
9. 9
10. 1010
11. 16cms^2
12. 24
13. octagon
14. 6000 or 6 thousands
15. 45

Answers Test 42

1. 21g
2. 1
3. one thousand and eighty-two
4. 12
5. 15
6. 29, 42, 53, 60, 126
7. 8
8. £1.60
9. 4
10. 42
11.
12. $^2/_6$, $^1/_3$
13. 250mls
14. 14
15. 6cms

Answers Test 43

1. one hundred and nineteen
2. 16
3. 101
4. 36
5. 5
6. 4
7. four thousand, three hundred and seventy-six
8. 130
9. 26
10. 58
11. $^1/_2$
12. 5hrs 15mins
13. 3,520
14. £1.00
15. 53

Answers Test 44

1. 101
2. 21
3. 15
4. 1729, 1927, 2917, 9172
5. 3
6. 8
7. 9
8. £1.17
9. 68
10. 114
11. pentagon
12. 7
13. 3
14. 31
15. 2hrs 45mins

Answers Test 45

1. 18
2. 10
3. 6
4. 6
5. 32
6. 40 or 4 tens
7. sixty
8. 36
9. 12
10. 1127
11. 50cms
12. $^2/_3$
13. 12
14. 7hrs 5mins
15. 30

Answers Test 46

1. 152
2. 11
3. £1.60
4. 12
5. 84
6. £1.05
7. two thousand, six hundred and seventy-five
8. 500
9. 3
10. 4
11. 6,300
12. 900 or 9 hundreds
13. 9
14. $^6/_{12}$, $^1/_2$
15. £13.65

Answers Test 47

1. 18
2. 4
3. 27
4. £1.99
5. 5
6. 2
7. 2,443
8. 9
9. 212
10. 20
11. 70cm^2
12. 8
13. 1
14. £8.86
15. 8,306

Answers Test 48

1. 17
2. 4
3. 56
4. 8
5. 3000 or 3 thousands
6. 3
7. six hundred and seventy-four
8. 24
9. 26
10. 58
11.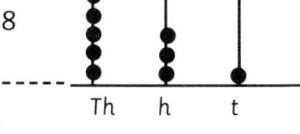
12. 7
13. NE
14. 9,006
15. 7

Answers Test 49

1. 20
2. 14
3. 4
4. 108
5. 9
6. 8
7. 9,000 or 9 thousands
8. 330
9. two thousand, four hundred and thirty-five
10. 111
11. 7,204
12. 7
13. 7.5
14. $7\frac{1}{2}$
15. 6

Answers Test 50

1. 19
2. 1230, 1340, 1350, 1450
3. 81
4. 10
5. 30
6. 8.8
7. $8\frac{4}{5}$ or $8\frac{8}{10}$
8. 4
9. 33
10. 15
11. 65
12. 15
13. 2,543
14. £7.90
15. 9hrs 24 mins

Answers Test 51

1. 22
2. 40
3. S.E.
4. 52p
5. 7p
6. 850mls
7. 12
8. 110
9. 100
10. 250
11. 56
12. 3.7
13. $3\frac{7}{10}$
14. 11p
15. 250.42

Answers Test 52

1. 90 or 9 tens
2. 4
3. $\frac{1}{3}$
4. 0.3 recurring
5. 9
6. 42
7. £3.87
8. £1.30
9. 80g
10. 8
11. 1.68m
12. 12
13. 17
14. 320.02
15. 8:00pm

Answers Test 53

1. 26
2. 8, 7
3. 72
4. 6
5. 48p
6. 17
7. 32
8. £3.68, £1.20, 95p, 67p
9. 2 or 2 units
10. 5
11. 0.5
12. 8
13. 4.7cms
14. 40cms
15. 75cms

Answers Test 54

1. 23
2. 10
3. 4hrs 35mins
4. 7
5. 26p
6. 19
7. two thousand, two hundred and fifty-six
8. 91
9. 6
10. 17
11. 415.03
12. 20 minutes
13. £1.36
14. 80 (approx)
15. 42

Answers Test 55

1. 23
2. thirteen
3. £1.08
4. 6
5. 1.44m
6. 19
7. 170
8. 20cms
9. two thousand, seven hundred and eighty-three
10. 900
11. 3.5kg
12. 40 mins
13. ---------

  h   t   u   tth hths
14. 11
15. 1/4

Answers Test 56

1. 4
2. 0
3. 3:30
4. Monday
5. 28
6. 72p
7. 9/1, 8/2, 7/3, 6/4 or 5/5
8. 8
9. 4
10. 111
11. between 600 - 800
12. 0.75
13. 2.60kms
14. 400miles
15. £1.14

Answers Test 57

1. 0
2. 28
3. no, it is odd
4. 10
5. 84
6. 10p
7. September
8. £1.08
9. 30
10. 9 times
11. 6
12. 143.13
13. 10 times
14. 900
15. 4.5kg

Answers Test 58

1. 21
2. 18cms
3. 5p
4. 6.8cms
5. 5yrs old
6. 20
7. 4
8. 36
9. 8
10. 8
11. $^1/_2$
12. £1.80
13. 48secs
14. 3
15. 3hrs 0mins

Answers Test 59

1. 19
2. 7
3. --------

  h   t   u   tth hths
4. 9
5. 50p
6. 100
7. 19p
8. 11, 10
9. 36
10. three thousand, one hundred and twenty-eight
11. 29
12. 48
13.

14. $^3/_4$
15. £3

Answers Test 60

1. 23
2. 2hrs 15mins
3. 30
4. £5.07
5. 6
6. £3.60
7. 128
8. 62mins
9. 17
10. 3 or 3 units
11. 4
12. 1.5l
13. 7.5cm
14. 351.21
15. $3^1/_2$

Answers Test 61

1. 26
2. 9
3. 17
4. 6
5. 14:15
6. 96
7. 3
8. 14
9. 9
10. 8:30am
11. 7m
12. 9.7
13. $9^7/_{10}$
14. $7^1/_4$
15. $^3/_5$

Answers Test 62

1. 48
2. 29
3. 12
4. 190
5. 200
6. 6
7. 3
8. 84
9. 20
10. hexagon
11. £88
12. 0.03
13. 203.42
14. 5mins
15. 23

Answers Test 63

1. 56
2. 15
3. one hundred and four
4. 20
5. 6,000 or 6 thousands
6. 4
7. 9
8. 20 more
9. 600 or 6 hundreds
10. 2
11. 144
12. 3.7cm
13. £31.29
14. 5.5kg
15. 500g

Answers Test 64

1. 46
2. 15
3. 4
4. 32
5. £1.31
6. 12
7. 7
8. 4
9. 4
10. S.W.
11. 8
12. yes
13.
14. 2/3
15. 1.2km

Answers Test 65

1. 230
2. 40
3. 8
4. 16cm²
5. 4
6. 12
7. 9
8. 4:40
9. 8,000 or 8 thousands
10. 44
11. 110 fish
12. $^3/_4$
13. 28
14. 180°
15. 103.24

Answers Test 66

1. 23
2. 110
3. 42
4. 9
5. 26p
6. 19
7. two thousand, two hundred and fifty-six
8. 91
9. 6
10. 17
11. -5°
12. 15°
13. 1.2m
14. £12
15. 6hrs

Answers Test 67

1. 9,704
2. 4
3. 5
4. 40
5. 20
6. 12
7. 72
8. 90 or 9 tens
9. 7
10. 8r3
11. 1.65
12. -11°C
13. yes
14. £7.83
15. -3

Answers Test 68

1. 10
2. 3:15
3. 25p
4. £5
5. 5r4
6. 9
7. 11
8. seven thousand, six hundred and five
9. 40
10. 21
11. 5
12. -3°C
13. 1, 2, 3, 5, 7
14. 3.45m
15. 1.5l

Answers Test 69

1. 4
2. 6r1
3. 60
4. 32
5. 25
6. 50
7. 11
8. 22
9. 1
10. 9
11. 2.5l
12. 6
13. 10
14. 56p
15. 250.54

Answers Test 70

1. two thousand, five hundred and ninety-six
2. 56,278
3. 135
4. 2.5kg
5. a century
6. 10
7. 72
8. 57
9. 8
10. 27
11. -7°C
12. 11, 13, 17, 19
13. -2
14. 32p
15. £10.50

Answers Test 71

1. 8.4
2. 32
3. 149
4. 9,000 or 9 thousands
5. 600 or six hundreds
6. 3.46m
7. 56
8.
9. £15.00
10. 72
11. $^1/_2$
12. 6
13. 5.8
14. 2°C
15. £25.20

Answers Test 72

1. 4
2. 86
3. 10
4. seven thousand, six hundred and six
5. 7, 8, 5
6. 9
7. 3hrs 35mins
8. 14
9. 64
10. 37
11. £2.14
12. -9°C
13. 6.5g
14. 12cms²
15. 14cms